Table of Contents

Introduction

The Myths and Legends

Myths are stories that give reasons for things. Some myths explain natural events such as rainbows or the seasons. Some myths tell how foods and agricultural tools were invented. Others explain how the world began. Myths about people and gods give reasons why people act the way they do. They are lessons that provide examples of good and bad behavior. Gods, goddesses, superhuman beings, and supernatural creatures such as Pegasus, the flying horse, are important in mythology.

A legend is a story that is not entirely invented. There may be plenty of exaggeration and fantasy in a legend, but at its heart there is some historical truth. Legends have heroes who perform great deeds with their strength and intelligence. Often heroes give up their dreams of happiness to help others. Their adventures can change the way they think and act.

All myths and legends are stories that were told and retold for hundreds or thousands of years before they were written down.

Ways to Use *Myths & Legends*

1. Directed lessons
   - with small groups of students reading at the same level
   - with an individual student

2. Partner reading

3. With cooperative learning groups

4. Independent practice
   - at school
   - at home

Things to Consider

1. Determine your purpose for selecting a story—instructional device, partner reading, group work, or independent reading. Each purpose calls for a different degree of story difficulty and support.

2. A single story may be used for more than one purpose. You might first use the story as an instructional tool, have partners read the story a second time for greater fluency, and then use the story at a later time for independent reading.

3. When presenting a story to a group or an individual for the first time, review any vocabulary that will be difficult to decode or understand. Many students will benefit from a review of the vocabulary page and the questions before they read the story.

Types of Skill Pages

Three or four pages of activities covering a wide variety of reading skills follow each story:

- comprehension
- vocabulary
- structural analysis
- figures of speech
- character analysis
- understanding plot development
- setting and mood

Ways to Use the Skill Pages

1. Individualize skill practice for each student with tasks that are appropriate for his or her needs.

2. As directed minilessons, the skill pages may be used in several ways:

   - Make a transparency for students to follow as you work through the lesson.

   - Write the activity on the board and call on students to fill in the answers.

   - Reproduce the page for everyone to use as you direct the lesson.

3. When using the skill pages for independent practice, make sure that the skills have been introduced to the reader. Review the directions and check for understanding. Review the completed lesson with the student to determine if further practice is needed.

Introduction to Greek and Roman Myths

The ancient Greeks, like many peoples, tried to explain the mysteries of nature and how things came to be. They lacked the scientific knowledge that we have today, so they created many gods and goddesses—powerful beings who rule storms, seasons, stars, the growing of things, love, death, and everyday life.

According to the Greek myths, the gods and goddesses lived on top of a mountain that was too high for people to climb. The mountain was called Olympus. The gods and goddesses often visited Earth, sometimes disguised as animals or people.

People built temples dedicated to these gods and goddesses. They left offerings and prayed in the temples for the help of the gods and goddesses. Often homes would have a shrine dedicated to a god or goddess.

As with all stories that are told, myths grew and changed through the years. Some of the Greek myths and legends were written as early as 750 to 700 B.C.

When the Romans conquered the Greeks, they took over the Greek gods and goddesses. They gave them Roman names.

Here are some of the names of Greek and Roman gods and goddesses and other characters mentioned in this book. Roman names are written in parentheses.

Aphrodite (Venus)–*the goddess of love and beauty*

Athena (Minerva)–*the goddess of wisdom and war*

Demeter (Ceres)–*the goddess of the harvest and the Earth*

Eros (Cupid)–*the god of love*

Hera (Juno)–*the queen of the gods and goddesses as well as the protector of women*

Hermes (Mercury)–*the messenger of the gods*

Medusa–*one of the three Gorgons, sisters with horrible faces and writhing snakes instead of hair*

Minotaur–*a creature who was half bull and half man*

nymphs–*female spirits of nature*

oracle–*a person or place where the gods and goddesses revealed truths to humans*

Persephone (Proserpina)–*helped her mother, Demeter (Ceres), care for the harvest and plants of the Earth*

Hades (Pluto)–*the king of the Underworld who ruled the dead*

Zeus (Jupiter)–*ruled Olympus; hurled thunderbolts when he was angry*

Arachne's Web

When the wind carried the sound of Arachne's spinning song to the villages and forests, people stopped their work. They came to admire her woven pictures. Even the nymphs from the forest sat at Arachne's feet and watched her hands card and spin delicate wool threads. All agreed that no other mortal could produce such beautiful weavings.

"You are second only to the goddess Minerva, the patron of weaving," said a nymph as she watched Arachne weave a picture of the creatures of the sea. "She has given you a special gift. No other mortal can do as well with the shuttle and needle. I can only guess that you visit Minerva's temple often and set out offerings to receive such blessings from her."

"Blessings from Minerva? I should say not!" answered Arachne. "You insult me with those words. My work, as you can see, is better than Minerva's. I could teach her the true art of weaving if she came here. Look what my needle can do. I embroider each scene. No one, goddess or mortal, can compare her work to mine."

Minerva, who heard Arachne's boasts, decided to teach Arachne a lesson. She disguised herself as an old woman, and, wrapped in a large cloak, paid a visit to the young woman's house. She stood behind Arachne, watching her work. After a time, she tapped her cane on the ground and hummed a little tune.

"Be off, old woman!" Arachne yelled. "Your noise breaks the rhythm of my song. I can't finish this picture if you continue to sing and tap your cane."

"It's just my way of admiring your work," answered the old woman. "Your picture is almost as beautiful as the weavings of the goddess Minerva. She would be proud that you have learned these skills from her. But it is said that you boast of being a better weaver than that goddess. Surely no mortal's work can compare with that of the gods. If you bring offerings to her altar and take back your words, I am sure that Minerva will forgive you and continue to bless your work."

"Old woman, don't talk to me about Minerva," answered Arachne. "If she were here at this time, she could see that I am a better weaver than all mortals and goddesses. If Minerva and I were to compete, it's clear that I would be the winner," answered Arachne. "Now leave me to my work."

5

"Old woman, you say!" Minerva threw off the cloak. "Look again and see who hears your words."

Arachne stood and drew back in fear when she saw Minerva. Even then, she didn't apologize or take back what she had said.

"If you insist, we shall have a contest and the nymphs will judge our work," challenged Minerva. "Beware! If you lose, you will pay for your boasts."

"I will not lose," answered Arachne. "You will see the beauty of my work. I will prove that I am the greatest weaver of all."

The two weavers set their looms. Their shuttles wove pictures of the gods and goddesses. Even in her designs, Arachne was boastful. She pictured the gods with angry, vengeful looks. She often stopped to see Minerva's tapestry. Minerva's weaving seemed so real that Arachne could hear the roar of the waves in her wind-swept sea. She showed the gods and goddesses on Mount Olympus looking lovingly down on the earth. It was a picture that was fine enough to decorate the walls of the house of the gods. Even so, Arachne believed her weaving was equal to Minerva's. The goddess worked so quickly that her hands were a blur. Arachne wove faster, trying to keep up with her.

Minerva and Arachne put down their shuttles just before sunset. The nymphs and all who watched the contest declared Minerva the winner. They agreed that Arachne's tapestry was a work of art, but in Minerva's weaving the sea, the earth, and the gods themselves seemed alive.

When Minerva saw the spiteful way Arachne had portrayed the gods, she ripped Arachne's tapestry and threw her shuttle at Arachne. The shuttle hit Arachne on the head. Immediately, Arachne began to change. She shriveled into a small, round shape. Four long, yarn-sized legs grew on each side of her body. Ashamed, Arachne scurried into a dark corner and hid under a chair.

Minerva threw a piece of webbing from Arachne's picture at the transformed woman. "Now you will pay for your boastful words. You will spin webbing for the rest of your life. You will never be able to add the colorful scenes you have pictured in the past. Here you will stay, hanging on the threads of your webbing forever."

Even today, all of Arachne's children spin webs in hidden corners. They move about attached to strands of webbing just as Arachne did. Their work is never finished. Only the web is set. No shuttle weaves scenes into their webs.

Name _____

1. What was Arachne's special talent?

   _____

2. Cite an example from the myth that supports this statement: Arachne held herself equal to the gods.

   _____

   _____

3. Which goddess did the Romans believe to be Arachne's patron?

   _____

4. Why did the two weavers have a contest?

   _____

5. What was the difference between the two finished tapestries?

   _____

   _____

6. What was the result of Arachne's disrespect?

   _____

   _____

7. What characteristics of the class of animals Arachnida are explained by this story?

   _____

   _____

Name _____

Arachne's Web
Comparing Two Characters

Write the descriptive words from the Word Box under the appropriate name. (Some words will be used for both characters.) Add words of your own. Then on another sheet of paper, use the lists to write a paragraph about each character. Finally, write a third paragraph comparing the two characters.

Arachne

_____ _____

_____ _____

_____ _____

_____ _____

Minerva

_____ _____

_____ _____

_____ _____

_____ _____

Word Box			
talented	forgiving	proud	confident
boastful	respectful	self-centered	indignant

Name _____

Arachne's Web
Vocabulary

A. Some common words take on special meanings when they are used in a specific context. *Weaving* is a good example of this. Write the number of each word by its meaning. Use the story context and/or a dictionary to help you.

1. shuttle

2. set the loom

3. card

4. spin

_____ to clean and comb raw wool

_____ a holder that carries the thread across the loom

_____ to draw out and twist into thread

_____ to put the warp threads on the loom

B. Use the words in the Word Box to complete the sentences.

Word Box		
transformed	tapestry	shriveled
vengeful	portrayed	delicate

1. The _____ _____ was the work of a master craftsman.

2. Her head was filled with _____ thoughts after the girls teased her.

3. When the fruit is removed from the dehydrator it is _____.

4. The new hairstyle and clean jeans _____ the worker.

5. The author _____ the teacher as an important influence on his life.

Name _____

Arachne's Web
Figurative Language

Sometimes a writer takes a word or phrase that has an obvious, literal meaning and uses it to create a word picture that has a different meaning.

Think about a spider spinning a web. Then read this sentence:

The conspirators wove an intricate **web of deceit.**

By comparing the conspirators' plan to a spider web, the writer creates an image of a complex network of connections.

Here are some phrases that can have both a literal and a figurative meaning. Use each phrase to create a word picture.

1. **hanging by a thread**
   Use this phrase in a sentence about someone whose job is in jeopardy.

   _____

   _____

2. **flying high**
   Use this phrase in a sentence about someone who just got an A⁺.

   _____

   _____

3. **building a bridge**
   Use this phrase in a sentence about two friends from different neighborhoods.

   _____

   _____

10

Echo and Narcissus

Echo played in the forests, entertaining the other nymphs with her stories and songs. Her voice was never silent. One day, the goddess Juno came into the forest looking for her husband, Jupiter. Echo stopped the goddess and began telling stories. She wouldn't stop talking. She followed wherever Juno went, telling her about all the nymphs in the forest.

Finally, Juno became so angry with the gossiping nymph that she took away the nymph's voice. "You will never again have the first word," the goddess said. "You will only be able to repeat the last words of those who speak to you."

Echo hid in caves near the mountains she had once loved to climb. She was ashamed to meet her friends and not be able to greet them. When the other nymphs called to her, she called back, repeating the last words they had said.

One day, Narcissus, a handsome youth, stopped to rest in the shade of a giant rock. Echo, who was hiding in a nearby cave, gazed upon the godlike young man and fell in love with him. But since Juno had taken away her first words, she had to wait for him to speak. She left the cave and sat down beside the young man.

Narcissus, who felt he was better than all others, frowned at Echo. "Why are you here?" he asked.

"Here," repeated Echo.

"I wish you would go away!" Narcissus said.

"Away," repeated Echo. She hid behind a tree and watched Narcissus.

Myths & Legends • EMC 759

Narcissus walked to a nearby pond to get a drink. When he bent down, he saw a beautiful face staring back at him. Narcissus smiled, and the face smiled at him. He tried to touch the face, but it disappeared under the water. Narcissus waited until the water was calm, then looked again. The face was there once more.

"I can see you care for me just as I care for you," said Narcissus to the face in the water. "When I smile, you return my smile. Still, you won't let me touch you. I will have to be content to stay here and gaze at your face. My heart is filled with love for you."

"Love for you," Echo repeated sadly, but Narcissus didn't seem to hear her. He just gazed at his own reflection in the pond. Narcissus had fallen in love with himself.

Narcissus was so much in love that he forgot to eat and drink. He grew pale and became ill. Even so, he didn't leave the face in the pond. Finally he died, and there, by the pond, a beautiful purple and white flower grew. The gods called the flower the narcissus in memory of the youth who loved only himself.

Echo mourned the handsome Narcissus. She died of grief, unable to tell anyone about her love. Her voice is still heard repeating the last words she hears.

Name _____

Questions about
Echo and Narcissus

1. What is the main characteristic of Echo?

_____

2. What happened as a result of that characteristic?

_____

_____

3. What is the main characteristic of Narcissus?

_____

4. What happened as a result of that characteristic?

_____

_____

5. Would you consider this myth a tragedy or a comedy? Justify your answer.

_____

_____

_____

_____

_____

Name _____

Echo and Narcissus
Word Origins

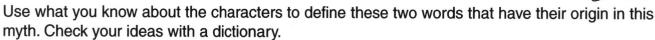

Use what you know about the characters to define these two words that have their origin in this myth. Check your ideas with a dictionary.

1. The words of the song will echo through the halls when the choir sings.

   Echo means _____

   _____

2. The psychologist said that the patient suffered from narcissism.

   Narcissism means _____

   _____

● ● ● Synonyms ● ● ●

Write the number of each word by its synonym.

1. quiet	_____ gazed
2. amusing	_____ mourned
3. recollection	_____ ashamed
4. spirit of nature	_____ content
5. scowled	_____ reflection
6. satisfied	_____ memory
7. stared at	_____ frowned
8. image	_____ silent
9. disgraced	_____ entertaining
10. grieved	_____ nymph

Name _____

Echo and Narcissus
Word Connotations

Many words have a **connotation** (a meaning that is suggested) as well as a dictionary definition. For example, *storyteller* has a positive connotation, while *gossip* has a negative connotation.

1. Write the words from the Word Box in the correct column.

Positive or Neutral Connotation   **Negative Connotation**

_____ _____   _____ _____

_____ _____   _____ _____

_____ _____   _____ _____

_____ _____   _____ _____

_____ _____   _____ _____

2. Write two pairs of words from the Word Box that are synonyms.

_____   _____

3. Write two pairs of words from the Word Box that are antonyms.

_____   _____

Word Box					
fragrance	odor	slanderous	conceited	lovely	nightmare
dream	ugly	opinionated	petite	generous	greedy
soiled	filthy	noteworthy	puny	famous	proud

Name _____

Echo and Narcissus

Only an Echo

Imagine that you could only repeat the last words of the person speaking to you. Write a story about an everyday happening with your echo responses.

_____

_____

_____

_____

_____

_____

_____

_____

_____

_____

_____

_____

_____

_____

Jason and the Golden Fleece

Jason walked through the marketplace. He had lost one sandal on the long journey to Iolcus and was searching for a new pair. Suddenly, soldiers and King Pelias himself rode their horses into the marketplace.

Pelias spoke. "Few strangers come to my kingdom. I have been warned by the prophets that a visitor with one shoe will come here to harm me."

"*Your* kingdom, dear Uncle?" Jason answered. "Don't you recognize me? I am your brother's son, Jason. I've come to take back the throne. Even though I was a young boy, I remember the agreement between you and my father. You were to rule until I was old enough to be king. I was sent to another kingdom to live until that time."

"I shall live up to my agreement, but how do you expect the people of Iolcus to follow your rule? They know nothing about you," responded Pelias. "You must win their trust by performing a brave deed. I will send you on a quest so that you can prove your bravery."

"There is some truth to your words," Jason answered. "What will you have me do?"

"There is a ram that was stolen from this country. Its magic Golden Fleece belongs here. If you go to the King of Colchis and demand the return of the fleece, you will be a hero. I will give up the throne if you are successful."

"I shall set out as soon as I build a ship," answered Jason.

Jason hired a master shipbuilder to build a ship for fifty rowers. It was the largest ship that had ever sailed the sea. Jason christened the ship *Argo.* He and his crew of strong warriors, the Argonauts, sailed away.

During the journey they stopped on an island to rest. There they found a man named Phineus being held captive by giant birds called Harpies. The Argonauts rescued Phineus. To thank Jason and his crew, Phineus warned him about the crashing islands that lay ahead.

"When you come to two rocky islands, one on each side of the sea, beware," Phineus said. "The islands crash together when ships sail between them. The ships and their crews are crushed. When you are close to the rocks, free this dove. The islands will come together when the dove flies between them. When the islands are moving apart again, you will be able to pass safely."

When the *Argo* reached the islands, Jason released the dove. The bird flew between the islands before they slammed together. Jason and his crew quickly rowed past the islands while they were opening up again.

When the Argonauts reached Colchis, the king refused to give up the Golden Fleece.

"You must earn your prize," he said. "First, Jason, you must harness my two fire-breathing bulls and plant my field with these teeth from a dragon. Each tooth will spring from the earth in the form of an armed warrior. You must slay each one as he appears."

It was an impossible task, but Jason decided he must try. It was the only way to regain his father's kingdom. In preparation, Jason offered prayers to the gods.

Hera, queen of the gods and goddesses, heard Jason's prayers and took pity on him. She asked Eros, the god of love, to shoot arrows into the heart of Medea, the daughter of the King of Colchis. When Medea was struck with the arrow of love, she fell in love with Jason. She gave him a magic charm and a special oil that would protect him from the flames of the bulls.

Jason charmed the fire-breathing bulls and hitched them to a plow. Then he sowed the dragon's teeth. He fought bravely, but the warriors who sprang from the ground overpowered him. Quickly he threw Medea's magic charm at them. They turned on each other and fought to the death.

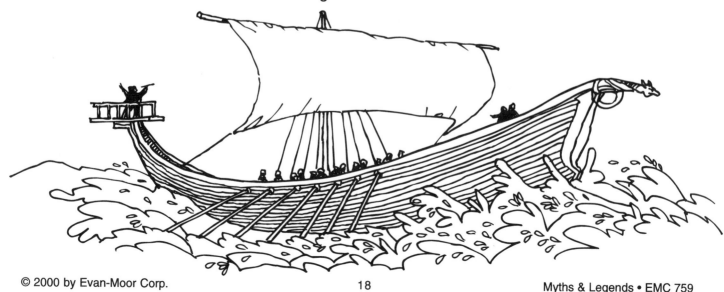

The next task was even more dangerous. Jason had to take the Golden Fleece away from a fierce dragon. Medea gave Jason a magic sleeping potion to pour on the dragon. When the dragon fell asleep, Jason stole the Golden Fleece and sailed away with Medea and the Argonauts.

When King Pelias heard that Jason and the Argonauts had returned with the Golden Fleece, he didn't welcome them. He refused to place the crown on Jason's head.

Medea tricked King Pelias's daughters into killing their father, saying that she would give them magic herbs that would bring Pelias back to life and make him young again so that he would always be with them. But the herbs Medea gave them were not magic, and Pelias was dead.

The people of Iolcus turned on Medea because of her evil deed, and refused to accept her as queen. Jason, too, spurned Medea and asked her to leave so that he could marry the Princess of Corinth. This made Medea so angry, she sent an enchanted robe to the princess. When the princess put it on, she went up in flames, along with the whole palace.

Grieving for his bride, Jason walked to where the *Argo* was resting on the sand and sat beside it. A sudden wind blew in from the sea. A mighty timber broke off the bow of the ship and fell on Jason, killing him.

The god Zeus sent the ship into the heavens to honor Jason's brave deeds. There it became the constellation Argo.

 Myths & Legends • EMC 759

Name _____

Questions about
Jason and the Golden Fleece

1. Why did Jason travel to the kingdom of King Pelias?

_____

_____

2. What did King Pelias want Jason to do?

_____

3. What was the real reason King Pelias gave Jason such an impossible quest?

_____

4. Name at least five smaller obstacles that Jason had to overcome while on his quest.

_____

_____

_____

_____

_____

5. Match the phenomenon with the magic that Jason used to conquer it.

crashing islands   oil

fire-breathing bulls   sleeping potion

fierce dragon   dove

warriors in the field   magic charm

Name _____

Jason and the Golden Fleece
Character Analysis

Tell whether you consider the characters listed below honest or dishonest. Give an example from the story to support your opinion.

	Honest	**Dishonest**	
Jason	☐	☐	
King Pelias	☐	☐	
Phineus	☐	☐	
King of Colchis	☐	☐	
Medea	☐	☐	

21   Myths & Legends • EMC 759

Name _____

Jason and the Golden Fleece
Retelling the Story

Complete the sentences to retell the story.

1. Jason shopped for _____ in the marketplace.

2. He met _____ and his soldiers.

3. _____ sent _____ on a quest.

4. Jason built a _____. He christened it _____.

5. Jason rescued _____ from the _____.

6. Phineas warned Jason about the _____.

7. The King of Colchis told Jason to _____

   and _____.

8. Medea fell in love with _____.

   She gave him a _____ and a _____.

9. Jason took the _____ from the dragon.

10. Jason returned but King Pelias refused to give him _____.

11. King Pelias's daughters _____.

12. The Princess of Corinth and the palace _____.

13. A mighty timber broke off the *Argo* and _____.

14. _____ sent the ship to the heavens to become a _____.

Name _____

Jason and the Golden Fleece
Vocabulary

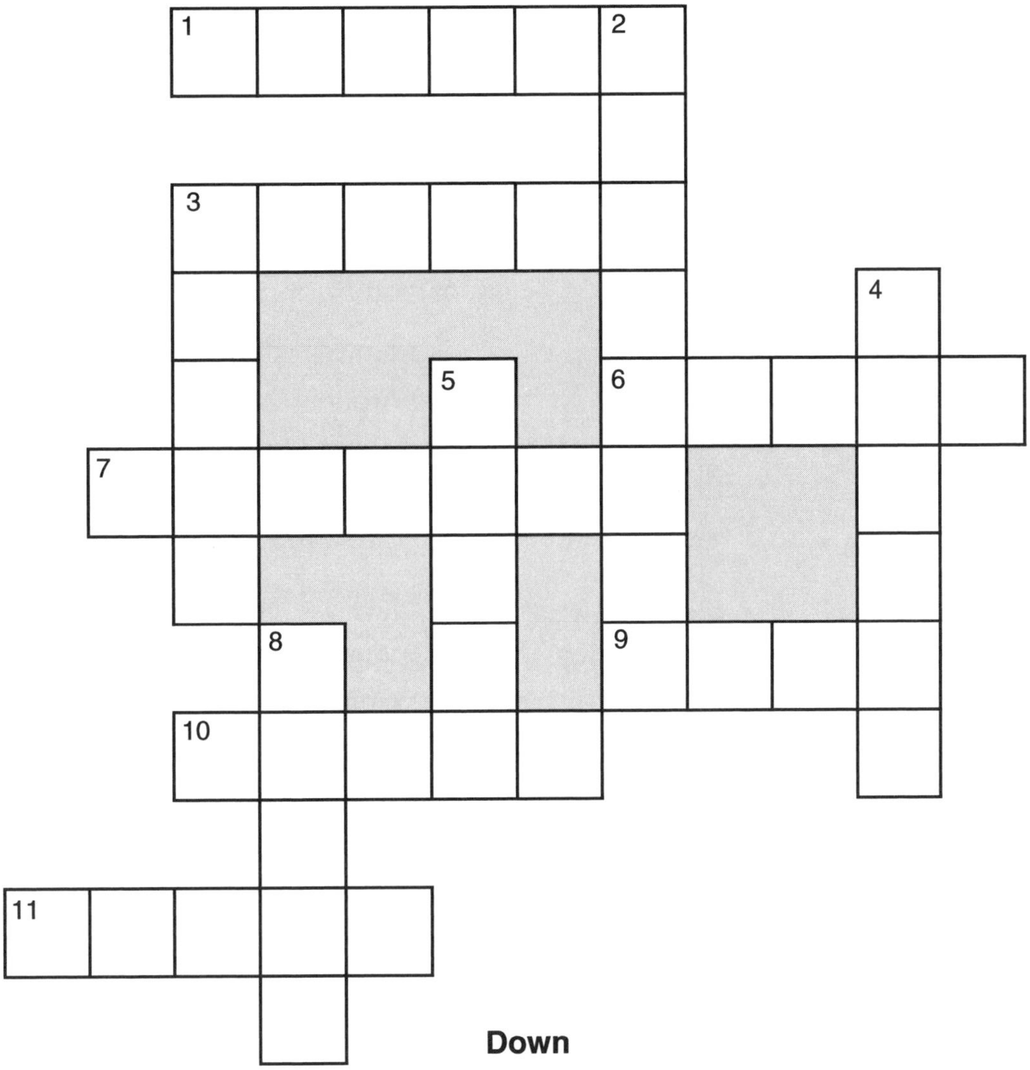

Across

1. It broke off the bow and killed Jason.

3. Jason lost one on his journey to Iolcus.

6. Eros shot one into the heart of Medea.

7. Jason offered _____ to the gods.

9. Phineas gave Jason one.

10. Another word for a search.

11. The King of Iolcus was Jason's _____.

Down

2. Jason _____ the dove.

3. To reject.

4. Jason went in search of the _____ Fleece.

5. Medea gave King Pelias's daughters magic _____.

8. Jason plowed the field with fire-breathing _____.

Myths & Legends • EMC 759

Orpheus and Eurydice

Orpheus was given the gift of music by the god Apollo. He played his magic lute wherever he wandered. Wild beasts rested peacefully with each other when they heard his songs. Birds in the forests sang with the lute and rested on his shoulders. Gods and mortals were enchanted by his music.

After he returned with Jason and the Argonauts from their quest for the Golden Fleece, Orpheus fell in love with the beautiful Eurydice. He serenaded her with love songs until she agreed to marry him.

On their wedding day, Eurydice danced across the meadow with the nymphs and muses while Orpheus played his lute. But alas, she stepped on a poisonous snake, and it bit her ankle.

Eurydice cried out in pain. Orpheus ran to her side, but he could not save her. She died and was taken to Hades' Land of the Dead. Orpheus mourned. His sad music brought tears to all who heard his songs.

Overcome with sorrow, Orpheus went to Zeus. He asked the god's permission to go to the Land of the Dead and beg Hades to release Eurydice.

Zeus cautioned him against the journey. "It's a dangerous place," he said. "No mortal has traveled to Hades' realm and returned to Earth."

"I will take that risk," Orpheus answered. "I would rather die there near Eurydice than live on Earth without her."

When Zeus could not persuade Orpheus to give up his quest, he reluctantly gave his permission for the journey.

           Myths & Legends • EMC 759

Orpheus traveled to the river Styx. He played his lute and sang about his beloved bride. The ferryman heard his song, and for the first time, he agreed to take a living mortal to the Land of the Dead. Orpheus continued to play as they made their way across the river. On the other side of the river, at the entrance to the Underworld, the dreaded four-headed dog that guarded Hades' realm stopped Orpheus. No living mortal had ever passed by him before. Orpheus played his songs and lulled the dog to sleep.

Orpheus made his way through caverns and passageways filled with lost souls. He played his lute and sang about his love for Eurydice. He brought happiness to many who had known no rest since they had arrived there. Everywhere he walked, he looked for Eurydice. Finally he came to the throne of Hades and Queen Persephone. He sang to them about his sorrow and asked for the release of Eurydice. Persephone cried when she heard his love songs. They reminded her of the spring flowers and sunlight in the world above them. The songs of Orpheus charmed even the King of the Underworld.

"You must listen carefully," said Hades. "I will see that Eurydice follows you back to the world, but you must not look at her until you have left my kingdom. If you do, she will return to my realm forever."

Orpheus made his way back through the passageways. He heard footsteps behind him. Orpheus wondered if Eurydice had changed since she entered the Kingdom of the Dead. Was she as beautiful as she had been on their wedding day? It didn't matter, of course. No matter what she looked like, Orpheus knew he would never love anyone else.

When Orpheus approached the end of the tunnel and saw sunlight ahead, he turned to call to Eurydice. Eurydice cried out when she saw his face, "Good-bye forever, fair Orpheus. Good-bye." Her hands reached out to him, but she disappeared back into the Realm of the Dead.

Orpheus tried to follow her, but he could not. Even his music didn't help him reenter Hades' kingdom. He lamented the foolishness that had caused Eurydice to be taken back by Hades. He called out, asking Hades to allow him to enter the Underworld again. The earth shook and Orpheus was transported back to the surface. He tried to find the river Styx, but he couldn't. The entrance to Hades' kingdom had closed up and there was no mark to show where it had been.

Orpheus continued to play his lute. His songs about the fate of the beautiful Eurydice were even sadder than before. The music brought tears to all who heard it. Orpheus wandered about the Earth from morning to night, playing his lute in the forests, hills, and towns.

A group of nymphs grew tired of Orpheus's sad songs. They mocked his grief and insisted that he dance with them. Orpheus paid no attention. The nymphs screamed so loudly that no one could hear his music. Still he didn't stop playing and singing.

Angry, the nymphs killed Orpheus and threw his body into a stream. His lute continued to play as it floated in the water. The muses found his body and transported him to the Land of the Dead. There he found Eurydice, and the two were reunited for eternity.

Name _____

Questions about
Orpheus and Eurydice

1. Summarize the story of Orpheus and Eurydice in four or five sentences.

_____

_____

_____

_____

_____

_____

2. What was it that enabled Orpheus to enter the Land of the Dead and charm Hades?

_____

3. Why do you think Orpheus looked back?

_____

_____

4. Do you think the story ended happily? Tell why or why not.

_____

_____

_____

27

Name _____

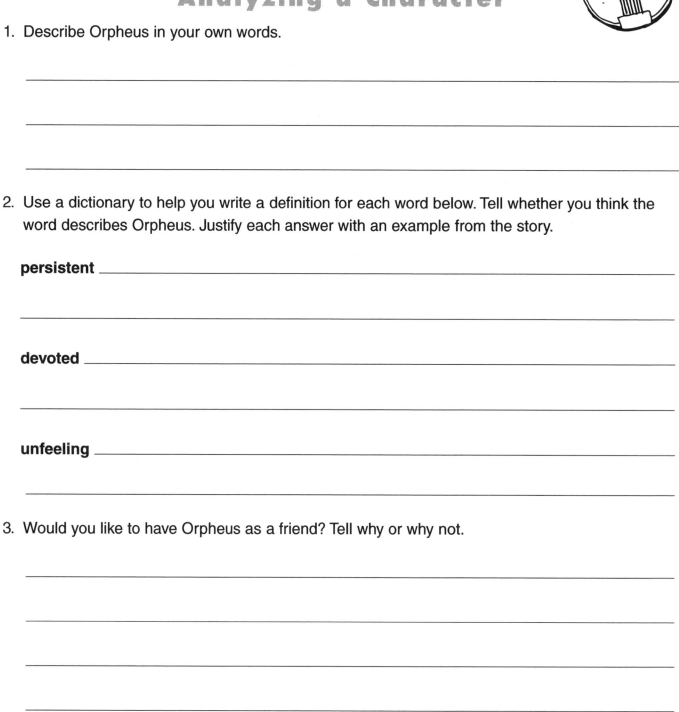

Orpheus and Eurydice
Analyzing a Character

1. Describe Orpheus in your own words.

_____

_____

_____

2. Use a dictionary to help you write a definition for each word below. Tell whether you think the word describes Orpheus. Justify each answer with an example from the story.

persistent _____

_____

devoted _____

_____

unfeeling _____

_____

3. Would you like to have Orpheus as a friend? Tell why or why not.

_____

_____

_____

_____

Name _____

Orpheus and Eurydice
Establishing Mood

In *Orpheus and Eurydice* many of the words used create a feeling of happiness or sadness.

1. Write the words from the Word Box in the correct column.

Happy Words	Sad Words
_____	_____
_____	_____
_____	_____
_____	_____
_____	_____
_____	_____

2. Which word is a synonym for *enchanted*? _____

3. Which word is a synonym for *mourned*? _____

Word Box			
cried	serenaded	lamented	happiness
enchanted	lulled	peace	sunlight
mourned	charmed	sorrow	foolishness

Name _____

Orpheus and Eurydice
Words with More Than One Meaning

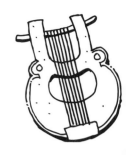

Use the words below to complete these sentences.

fair   mark   release

1. The referee helps to keep the contest _____.

2. _____ is another word for *grade*.

3. He pulled the _____ to open the cockpit.

4. My grandmother's quilt won first prize at the _____.

5. Orpheus searched in vain for some _____ that would help him find the river Styx.

6. Hades agreed to _____ Eurydice under certain conditions.

● ● ● Synonyms ● ● ●

Write the number of each word by its synonym.

1. fate   _____ search

2. persuade   _____ convince

3. realm   _____ kingdom

4. quest   _____ warned

5. cautioned   _____ destiny

Pandora

When the gods created Pandora, each gave her a special gift. They blessed her with great beauty and happiness. When they finished, the gods agreed that she was almost perfect. She would bring joy to all who lived on the Earth.

"Wait," a goddess said. "There is another gift she must have. If she doesn't want to learn about all the creatures on Earth and all she sees there, she will be bored." So the goddess added curiosity to Pandora's gifts.

Before Pandora left the house of the gods, she was given a chest that was tied and locked. Jupiter cautioned her, "Whatever happens, do not open the chest. Keep it locked forever. The contents will bring great unhappiness to the world."

On Earth, Pandora was loved and admired by everyone. Her laughter and song charmed the birds and animals in the forests. She chose the handsome Epimetheus as her husband. They lived a happy life, dancing and singing with their friends. The chest sat undisturbed in a corner of their house. When visitors came, they commented on the beautiful carvings of the gods that decorated the lid. Many asked to see the inside of the chest, but Pandora explained that it was a gift from the gods that was never to be opened.

"A gift from the gods?" said one. "Then of course it must hold great magic or priceless jewels. No chest should be closed forever."

Another nodded in agreement. "Surely one quick look would do no harm. No one would know—not even the gods themselves."

Pandora began to dream about the chest. Many times when she rubbed it with olive oil and polished it, her hands rested on the cord that held it closed. Once she loosened some of the knots. But before she could untie them, she heard Epimetheus entering the house.

"You spend hours polishing that chest. You think of nothing else," Epimetheus said. "It's better to forget the chest and come walk with us in the forest. We have finished our work for the day. Listen. You can hear the pipes calling everyone to dance."

"It's true," Pandora thought. "I must forget about the chest. Dreaming about it has made me very unhappy."

Pandora left the house with Epimetheus to enjoy the last warm rays of the afternoon sun. But even when she danced, she couldn't forget the chest. While the others ate their evening meal under the trees in the olive grove, Pandora went back to the house. "Just one look," she thought, "and then I'll know. After that I will put it aside and not worry about the treasures inside. If I leave it open for a moment, what harm could come of that?"

Pandora hurried to the chest. She loosened the knots and took a key from the shelf near the chest. Slowly she turned the lock. There were voices coming from inside the chest. "Hurry, Pandora. We have been waiting a long time."

Pandora moved away from the chest. "Who have the gods placed inside the chest?" she wondered. "Surely I didn't hear Jupiter correctly. Perhaps he meant to tell me to open the chest and free the poor creatures inside when I came to Earth." Pandora went back to the chest and worked the key in the lock. When she heard it click, she raised the lid and looked inside. A cloud of biting, stinging insects poured out. Their names were Sorrow, Pain, Evil, Greed, Envy, Despair, Hatred, Poor Health, Distrust, Laziness, and Lies.

Pandora slammed the chest shut, but it was too late. All the Furies had flown out of the chest. They swarmed about Pandora, biting her. She felt angry for the first time in her life. Before she could catch the creatures, they flew out the door and began to attack Epimetheus and his friends.

Epimetheus ran into the house to see if Pandora was safe. "I couldn't wait any longer!" Pandora cried. "I had to open the chest. There were voices inside calling to me. Look what I have done! All who live on Earth will suffer. The gods will never forgive me."

As Pandora sobbed in Epimetheus's arms, she heard another voice coming from the chest. "Pandora, open the chest once more."

"I will not open the chest again. Look what has happened," said Pandora. "There will never be a day of peace on Earth again."

"Pandora," called the voice in the chest. "You must let me out. I am the only one who can help."

"Perhaps you should look inside one more time," said Epimetheus. "It seems that all the harm that can be done has escaped from the chest."

"Pandora," called the voice again. "I will die if I'm left in this chest, and only the Furies will be left to inflict their sorrow on people. Open the chest and I will fly out into the world and end the suffering."

Pandora put her hands on the lid of the chest. She looked at Epimetheus. He nodded, and she opened the chest once more.

A tiny, winged creature flew from the box and perched on Pandora's shoulder. "I am Hope," it said. "When the Furies have caused their harm, I alone can take away the pain. I will fly to all who need my comfort, and they will live in peace once more."

Pandora wiped away her tears, and she and Epimetheus carried Hope out into the world.

Name _____

Questions about
Pandora

1. What was special about Pandora?

_____

2. How did Jupiter caution Pandora when she left the house of the gods?

_____

3. How did Pandora's feelings about the box change?

_____

4. What advice did Epimetheus give Pandora?

_____

5. What happened when Pandora opened the box?

_____

6. What one story event changed the ending so that it was not disastrous?

_____

7. Do you think the gods forgave Pandora? Tell why you think as you do.

_____

_____

_____

_____

Name _____

Pandora
Foreshadowing

Authors use **foreshadowing** to help readers know what is going to happen in a story. It is the same as leaving clues for the reader.

1. What warning did Jupiter give to Pandora?

_____

_____

2. How could this warning be considered foreshadowing?

_____

_____

_____

••• Understanding a Figure of Speech •••

1. There is an expression we use today that comes from this story. Sometimes people may describe something as a "Pandora's box." What do you think this expression means?

_____

_____

2. Think of one or more situations that might be described as a "Pandora's box."

_____

_____

_____

_____

Name _____

Pandora
Symbolism

A. A storyteller sometimes **symbolizes** an idea or an emotion by comparing it to something else, or giving it another form.

1. The storyteller describes what happens when Pandora opens the box, saying, "A cloud of biting, stinging insects poured out." What are the insects symbols of?

_____

2. Later the storyteller extends the symbolism. Tell the two things that are being compared in these sentences.

> A tiny, winged creature flew from the box and
> perched on Pandora's shoulder. "I am Hope," it said.

_____

B. Think of some interesting comparisons or symbols for the things below. List them in the boxes.

pain	greed	joy
_____	_____	_____
_____	_____	_____
_____	_____	_____
_____	_____	_____

Use one of the comparisons to write an interesting sentence.

_____

_____

Psyche and Cupid

So beautiful was Psyche that all who saw her compared her to Venus, the goddess of love. People threw flowers in Psyche's path and worshipped her as if she were a goddess.

Venus was angry to have her beauty compared to that of a mortal. She ordered her son, Cupid, to give Psyche a potion that would cause her to fall in love with a terrible monster.

That night Cupid carried a cup of sorrow and love to the palace where Psyche slept. As he washed her face with the potion, he saw her brow wrinkle with pain. "I cannot destroy anyone this beautiful," he said.

In his haste to wash away the sorrow, one of Cupid's arrows of love tumbled out of its quiver and pierced his foot. In that instant, he fell in love with Psyche. When Psyche awoke, Cupid told her, "My mother must not know about my love for you." And he flew away.

The next day, Venus saw that Psyche was still as happy as before. The angry goddess sent all the misfortunes that mortals can suffer to afflict Psyche.

Psyche's parents consulted an oracle to see what could be done for their daughter. They were told that Psyche would become the bride of a creature who was not mortal—that she would marry a monster.

One day while Psyche was climbing a high hill, Venus placed a slippery rock in her path. When Psyche stepped on the rock, she fell and tumbled down the steep slope. Cupid called to the wind to save his beloved Psyche. The wind caught her and laid her gently on a flowering meadow where she fell asleep.

When Psyche awoke, she saw a beautiful palace. She went inside and was given all she wished to have. She talked to voices, but never saw the servants who waited on her.

That night, when the palace was dark, Psyche heard another voice. The man's voice told her how much he loved her. She felt great joy when she heard the voice. Every night the voice returned.

 Myths & Legends • EMC 759

After months had passed, Psyche agreed to marry the mysterious visitor. At his request, she promised she would never try to look at his face. Her new husband came each night and disappeared before dawn.

Psyche's husband was kind. They laughed and sang together. He told her stories about the gods.

After a year had passed, Psyche said, "Please let my family visit. I'm lonely when you're away."

"They will bring you nothing but sorrow," he said.

Psyche persisted. Each night she begged to see her family. Her husband finally agreed. He asked the wind to bring her two sisters.

The two sisters were amazed when they saw the palace. "Your husband," asked the younger one, "is he as handsome as he is kind and generous?"

Psyche tried to ignore the questions, but her sisters continued to ask what her husband looked like.

Finally Psyche said, "I cannot tell you what he is like because he only comes at night and will not show his face."

"Then he must be a horrible monster, just as the oracle predicted," said the younger sister. "Otherwise he would let you see him."

 Myths & Legends • EMC 759

The older of the two sisters said, "When he returns, take a candle and a knife. Look at his face while he is sleeping. If he is a monster, you must destroy him before he kills you."

Psyche agreed and told the wind to carry her sisters home.

That night, while her husband slept, Psyche took a knife and a lighted candle to his bed. She stared down at her husband's handsome face and his wings. He wasn't mortal or a monster. He was the god Cupid! A drop of hot wax fell on Cupid's shoulder, waking him. Seeing the knife, he flew off.

Suddenly a fierce wind rocked the palace, and it disappeared. Psyche then began to wander the Earth looking for Cupid. She asked the goddess Ceres for help. Ceres told her to go to Venus and ask her forgiveness.

The goddess was not easily swayed. She stared at Psyche sternly and said, "Cupid is ill because you betrayed him. He sleeps and doesn't talk to anyone. If you wish to help him, you must complete the tasks I give you."

Psyche agreed to do Venus's bidding. Her first task was to sort the grains in the goddess's storehouse by evening. Psyche looked at the barley, wheat, and millet scattered on the floor. She couldn't finish in time. An ant, seeing her sorrow, brought all his friends to help. The grains were separated before the sun set.

For each of the impossible tasks that Venus gave Psyche, Ceres sent the creatures of the Earth to help Psyche.

All her tasks completed, Psyche searched until she found Cupid's room. She told him about the tasks Venus had given her and begged him to forgive her.

Cupid went to the great god Jupiter and asked for his help. Jupiter convinced Venus that the love Cupid and Psyche shared was too great to be destroyed. At Jupiter's insistence, Venus promised to let Psyche and Cupid live in peace.

Name _____

Questions about
Psyche and Cupid

1. How did Venus feel about Psyche? What happened as a result of Venus's feelings?

_____

_____

2. How did Cupid feel about Psyche? What happened as a result of Cupid's feelings?

_____

_____

3. What did the oracle foretell about Psyche's future?

_____

4. Describe the life that Psyche and her mysterious husband lived.

_____

_____

5. Why did Cupid fly off after Psyche saw his face?

_____

6. How did Psyche prove her love for Cupid?

_____

_____

_____

Name _____

Psyche and Cupid
Tracking Story Events

Complete the story map.

Psyche was climbing a high hill.

Venus _____.

Psyche _____.

Cupid _____.

The wind _____.

When Psyche awoke, she saw _____.

At night Psyche _____.

Psyche married _____.

What caused this happy situation to change?

_____

_____

Name _____

Psyche and Cupid
Vocabulary

A. Write each word below on the line in front of its meaning.

      mortal   potion   sorrow   haste

      quiver   oracle   insistence   generous

1. _____ gives freely

2. _____ a human being

3. _____ sadness

4. _____ hurry

5. _____ a constant demand

6. _____ a person or thing able to give wise guidance

7. _____ a carrying case for arrows

8. _____ a liquid medicine or drug

B. Use the words in the list above to complete these sentences.

1. Cupid didn't want to cause Psyche any _____.

2. Cupid was a _____ husband.

3. In his _____, Cupid lost an arrow from his

_____.

4. Jupiter's _____ made Venus change her mind.

            Myths & Legends • EMC 759

The Adventures of Perseus

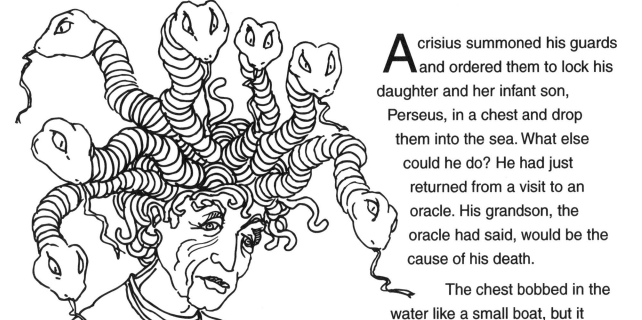

Acrisius summoned his guards and ordered them to lock his daughter and her infant son, Perseus, in a chest and drop them into the sea. What else could he do? He had just returned from a visit to an oracle. His grandson, the oracle had said, would be the cause of his death.

The chest bobbed in the water like a small boat, but it didn't sink. A boatman, on his way to Seriphus, pulled the chest from the water. He freed the mother and son and took them to Polydectes, the king of that country. The kindly king cared for them until Perseus was a young man.

To repay Polydectes for his care, Perseus vowed to kill the monster Medusa who threatened Polydectes' kingdom. Once a beautiful woman, Medusa had bragged that she was more beautiful than the goddess Minerva. Minerva changed Medusa's flowing hair into a halo of poisonous serpents. No living creature could look at Medusa's head without turning to stone.

Minerva decided to help the young hero. She gave Perseus a shield, a sword, and a bag. "When you find Medusa," she said, "look at her reflection in my shield. If you look directly at her, you will be turned to stone. Carry her head in this bag so no innocent people will see her."

The god Mercury gave Perseus his winged shoes so he could travel to Medusa's cave by air.

When Perseus reached Medusa's cave, he waited until the monster was resting. He searched the cave until he saw her image reflected in Minerva's shield. When the snakes saw him they made a loud hissing sound, waking Medusa. Perseus kept his eyes on Medusa's reflection in the shield. When she lunged toward him, he struck with Minerva's sword, cutting off Medusa's head. Without looking directly at Medusa, Perseus dropped her head into the bag.

Perseus flew over the country ruled by Atlas, a giant with amazing strength. Perseus looked down on the farms and orchards. Atlas's sheep and cattle were larger than anyone else's. Golden fruit growing in his orchards glowed in the afternoon sunlight. Even the branches of the trees were gold.

Tired from his journey, Perseus landed and found the giant tending his crops. "I am the son of the god Jupiter," said Perseus. "I have slain the mighty Medusa. I ask for food and rest."

Atlas was afraid Perseus would steal the precious golden apples from his orchard. "I do not believe you come as a friend. You are here to rob me of my treasures," the giant said. He reached out, trying to take hold of Perseus.

Perseus knew he could not win a fight against the strong giant. He took Medusa's head from the bag and held it toward Atlas. The giant changed into a gigantic stone mountain. The gods put Atlas's strength to work holding up the stars and the heavens.

After Perseus rested, he flew on across the sea. When he looked down, he saw a young woman chained to a rock. He landed next to her and broke the chains with Minerva's sword. "Who has done this terrible deed?" Perseus asked.

"My own mother, Queen Cassiopeia, and my father, the king. They had no choice. In order to save the kingdom from a cruel sea serpent, they were told they must sacrifice me to the monster."

At that moment the serpent rose up out of the sea. It blew red clouds of fire into the air. Andromeda, the young woman, screamed and clung to Perseus.

Perseus unsheathed his sword and gave Andromeda the shield for protection. He flew above the sea monster, jabbing his sword into its tough, scaly hide. He darted about, avoiding the monster's jagged fangs. Dying from the sword wounds, the monster sank into the sea.

Myths & Legends • EMC 759

The king and queen embraced their daughter and Perseus when they reached the castle. Because Perseus had rescued Andromeda, her parents offered her hand in marriage. The wedding and banquet were held the following day.

During the feast, the uninvited Phineus and his friends entered the banquet hall. "Andromeda was promised to me," Phineus said. "Perseus shall not take my bride."

"You gave up all rights to my daughter when you didn't rescue her from the sea monster," the king said. "Be gone!"

Phineus and his friends attacked Perseus and the other guests. At first, Perseus was able to defend Andromeda, but Phineus and his friends outnumbered the wedding party. They surrounded the bride and fought off Perseus and others who tried to rescue her.

Perseus grabbed Minerva's bag and called to all around him. "If you are a friend, close your eyes and look away. Don't be afraid. I will stop Phineus."

Perseus held up Medusa's head. Instantly Phineus and his friends became statues. With the fighting ended, the wedding feast continued. Andromeda and Perseus danced around the statues to celebrate their marriage.

Myths & Legends • EMC 759

Name _____

Questions about
The Adventures of Perseus

1. Why did Perseus set out on his adventures?

   _____

2. What help did Perseus receive?

   _____

3. Who were the four formidable enemies Perseus defeated in this myth?

   _____

4. Do you think Perseus used the head of Medusa responsibly? Tell why or why not.

   _____

   _____

5. Which of Perseus's weapons do you think was the most valuable? Support your answer with examples from the myth.

   _____

   _____

   _____

6. Was Perseus a hero? Write a persuasive paragraph in support of your answer.

   _____

   _____

   _____

   _____

Name _____

The Adventures of Perseus
Vocabulary

Some of the action verbs found in *The Adventures of Perseus* are given in the Word Box.
Complete the sentences below using these verbs. Then write a simple definition for each one.

1. The seamstress _____ the pins into the cushion.

_____

2. The principal _____ the student.

_____

3. The still water _____ the image.

_____

4. The grandmother _____ her grandson.

_____

5. The girl _____ the barking dog.

_____

6. The runner _____ about his victory.

_____

7. The juror _____ to tell the truth.

_____

8. The fencer _____ at his opponent.

_____

Name _____

The Adventures of Perseus
Verbs and Nouns

A. The same word can sometimes be used as a noun and a verb. Write *noun* or *verb* to identify the use of the underlined word in each sentence.

1. Minerva gave Perseus a <u>shield</u>. _____

2. <u>Shield</u> your face from Medusa's gaze. _____

3. Perseus knew that he could not win the <u>fight</u>. _____

4. I do not wish to <u>fight</u>. _____

5. I will <u>treasure</u> your daughter forever. _____

6. You are here to rob me of my <u>treasure</u>. _____

7. They must <u>sacrifice</u> me to the monster. _____

8. Queen Cassiopeia made a <u>sacrifice</u> to the sea serpent. _____

B. Write your own sentences. Use each word below as a verb in one sentence and as a noun in another sentence.

1. **work**

   verb– _____

   noun– _____

2. **drop**

   verb– _____

   noun– _____

3. **look**

   verb– _____

   noun– _____

 Myths & Legends • EMC 759

Name ____________________________

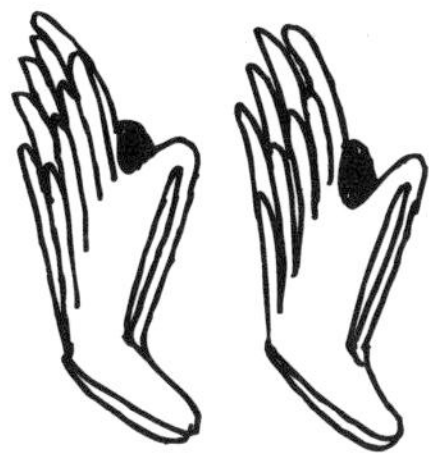

The Adventures of Perseus

Describing a Character

List character traits that describe each character. Then write a sentence about the character that synthesizes your ideas.

Medusa: • ______ • ______ • ______	**Atlas**: • ______ • ______ • ______
Sea Serpent: • ______ • ______ • ______	**Perseus**: • ______ • ______ • ______

The Seasons

Ceres, the sister of Jupiter, was the goddess of the Earth and all the plants and crops that grew there. She was kind to the families who farmed the Earth and helped them care for the land.

Ceres loved her daughter, the beautiful Proserpina, more than anything else. While Ceres went about her work, Proserpina gathered bouquets of flowers. Everywhere Proserpina walked, flowers bloomed. Her laugh brought joy to everyone.

One day Pluto, the god of the Underworld, saw Proserpina dancing in the meadow. He fell in love with her and wished to marry her. Even though his realm was large and filled with gold and precious stones, he knew Ceres would never allow Proserpina to journey to his faraway kingdom.

Pluto decided to kidnap Proserpina and carry her off to the Underworld. Surely, he reasoned, when she saw how kind he could be, she would fall in love with him and agree to marry him. Then she could rule happily as Queen of the Dead and brighten his dreary days.

Pluto used his magic powers to create a beautiful flower that was like no other. He set the flower in the earth at the edge of the woods. Hidden by the trees, Pluto waited with his horses and golden chariot.

Proserpina ran toward the flower, intending to add it to her basket. When she knelt to look at the flower, Pluto raced by. He gathered her up in his arms, and his chariot sped off, circling the Earth.

Myths & Legends • EMC 759

Proserpina's screams echoed through the woods. The nymphs hurried to see what was wrong. Pluto opened a chasm in the earth and drove his chariot underground. The ground closed overhead, leaving no trace of Proserpina. Pluto's chariot was gone by the time the nymphs reached the clearing.

When the sun was setting, Ceres came to find her daughter. She searched for her, frantically calling her name. The wood nymphs told her they heard Proserpina's screams but they didn't see what happened.

Night and day, Ceres searched the Earth, calling for her daughter. She forgot to care for the Earth. The ground dried and all the plants turned brown. Farmers begged Ceres to care for the Earth again, but she didn't hear them. Weeping, she continued to search for her daughter.

Ceres returned to the place where her daughter was last seen. A water nymph gave Ceres a jeweled belt that had been left by a stream.

"I found Proserpina's belt," she said. "Perhaps the sun saw what happened."

Ceres went to the sun and asked for help. The sun told her that Pluto had taken Proserpina to the Underworld.

Ceres hurried to see Jupiter in the Hall of the Gods. He told her that she must stop mourning for Proserpina. "Tend to the Earth," he said. "All mortals suffer because you no longer care for the plants and crops. When nothing grows, people can't leave food offerings in our temples. They will forget about us."

"I can't do my work when I think of my poor Proserpina hidden away under the ground," said Ceres. "My child, who loves the sun and flowers, will be miserable in Pluto's dark caverns."

 Myths & Legends • EMC 759

"Pluto rules over a large kingdom," said Jupiter. "His storerooms are filled with gold and jewels. He will be a good husband. Proserpina is fortunate."

"I can't be so far away from my beautiful Proserpina," Ceres answered. "If I am to care for the Earth again, I must have her back."

"Very well," said Jupiter. "I will send the messenger Mercury to fetch her. I warn you, if she has eaten any food in the World of the Dead, she will not be able to stay with you."

Mercury took the message to Pluto. The Underworld king knew that Proserpina cried for the sun and flowers. She would not eat, laugh, or sing. Sadly, Pluto allowed Proserpina to return to her mother. Before she left, he offered her the juice from sweet pomegranate seeds. Happy to be on her way back to Earth, Proserpina took the juice.

As Ceres greeted Proserpina with open arms, the flowers and plants began to grow around them.

"I feared you had eaten food in the Kingdom of the Dead and couldn't be returned to me," Ceres said. "Those who eat there must stay."

Proserpina cried out, "Mother, I didn't eat until I was certain I would be free to return to you, and it was no more than the juice from a few pomegranate seeds!"

Ceres rushed Proserpina to Jupiter and told him what she had done. "If she is sent back to the Underworld, I will not care for the Earth," she said.

Jupiter said, "Proserpina cannot remain on Earth all year because she took the juice. She will spend half the year with you and return to Pluto for the rest of the year."

Thus it is that when spring comes, Proserpina visits her mother. Then Ceres blesses the Earth. Flowers bloom and the crops are abundant. During the long, dark winter months, Ceres grieves and forgets to care for the Earth.

Myths & Legends • EMC 759

Questions about
The Seasons

1. What natural phenomenon is explained in this myth?

_____

2. What was Pluto's plan?

_____

3. What happened when Ceres forgot to care for the Earth?

_____

4. Why couldn't Proserpina return to the Earth to live?

_____

_____

5. Is Pluto an evil character in this myth? Support your answer with examples from the story.

_____

_____

_____

6. Do you think Jupiter's judgment about where Proserpina would stay was fair? Tell why or why not.

_____

_____

_____

_____

Name _____

The Seasons
Vocabulary

A. Write each word below on the line in front of its meaning.

chasm   precious   dreary   chariot   frantically

pomegranate   grieves   offerings   cavern   tend

1. _____ of great value   6. _____ to care for

2. _____ a large cave   7. _____ gifts

3. _____ gloomy   8. _____ mourns

4. _____ a tropical fruit   9. _____ wildly

5. _____ a deep opening   10. _____ two-wheeled,
                                                                 horse-drawn vehicle

B. Choose words from the list above to complete these sentences.

1. Winter is a time when Ceres is _____ because her _____

   daughter stays in the _____ _____ of the Underworld.

2. Pluto's _____ drove through the _____ in the earth.

3. Ceres forgets to _____ the flowers when she _____.

The Seasons
Categorizing Events

What seasonal occurrences would you classify as Ceres' blessings? Which ones could be classified as Ceres' forgetfulness? Fill in the chart below to answer the questions.

Ceres' Blessings	Ceres' Forgetfulness
_____	_____
_____	_____
_____	_____
_____	_____
_____	_____
_____	_____
_____	_____
_____	_____
_____	_____

Name _____

The Seasons
Creative Writing

Imagine that you are Proserpina. Write a letter to your mother from the Underworld. Tell about your surroundings, Pluto, and the things you miss about Earth.

Theseus and the Minotaur
&
Daedalus and Icarus

King Minos of Crete called for his royal architect and inventor, Daedalus. He knew that Daedalus was the only person clever enough to build a prison that could hold the dreaded Minotaur, a monster with a human body and the head of a bull. The Minotaur roamed about the kingdom, killing and eating the people of Crete. No one, not even the king, was safe.

Daedalus built a labyrinth that surrounded the Minotaur. The passageways were designed with twists and turns that seemed to have no end. Once inside the labyrinth, the Minotaur couldn't find the way out. Only Daedalus knew how to escape.

After the Minotaur was imprisoned, its hungry roars kept people awake at night. King Minos had to find a way to quiet the Minotaur so people could live in peace. He sent a message to King Aegeus of Athens. He demanded hostages from Athens to feed the Minotaur. Aegeus knew that he had no choice. King Minos's army was much stronger than his. He was forced to send fourteen youths and maidens to feed this monster.

Theseus, an Athenian hero and the son of King Aegeus, volunteered to go with the hostages. If he could kill the Minotaur, no more Athenians would have to be sent to Crete.

When Ariadne, King Minos's daughter, saw the handsome prisoner, Theseus, she fell in love with him. She asked Daedalus to help Theseus slay the Minotaur and then help him escape from the labyrinth. Ariadne gave Theseus a magic ball of string.

Ariadne told Theseus she would help him if he would take her back to Athens and marry her. Theseus, in love with the beautiful princess, agreed.

57

Theseus entered the labyrinth when the Minotaur was sleeping. He set the magic string Adriadne had given him on the ground. It rolled in front of him, leading him to the snoring monster. Theseus surprised the Minotaur and killed it. After his victory, Theseus followed the string to the entrance of the labyrinth.

Ariadne and Theseus freed the other prisoners and set sail for Athens.

On the way, the god Dionysus came to Theseus. The god wished to marry Ariadne, and told Theseus to leave her on the island of Naxos.

Although Theseus loved Ariadne, he had to obey the god's command. When Ariadne fell asleep, the broken-hearted Theseus left her on the island and then sailed on to Athens.

King Minos knew that Daedalus was the only one clever enough to help Theseus escape the labyrinth. He blamed Daedalus for the loss of his daughter, and locked him and his son Icarus in a high tower.

"King Minos controls the land and the sea," Daedalus said to his son, "so we must leave by air."

Daedalus made a giant set of bird's wings from feathers set in wax. He strapped them to his arms and soared through the air. Next he set about making wings for his son. The boy gathered feathers and helped his father fasten the feathers to the wax.

Daedalus, like a mother bird teaching her young, taught Icarus to fly. After a few days of practice, the boy could soar across the sky.

"We will set out when the sun rises," said Daedalus. "Heed my warning, Icarus. Follow close behind me. Whatever you do, don't sail too close to the sun."

The next morning, they strapped the wings on their outstretched arms and flew off over the sea.

Late in the afternoon, Icarus felt chilled by the sea breezes. He flew a little closer to the sun. The warmth made him feel much better. Forgetting his father's warning, he soared higher. When he was close to the sun, the wax holding the feathers in place melted. The feathers drifted down to the sea. Icarus, moving his arms back and forth, struggled. He called out to his father, but the wind swallowed his words. Icarus fell into the sea and, being mortal, drowned.

Daedalus, tired from the long flight, decided it was time to find a landing place and rest for the night. He looked behind him. Icarus was gone! Below him, he saw the feathers from Icarus's wings floating on the water. His son had fallen into the sea.

Daedalus landed on a nearby island. Grieving, he named the great sea the Icarian Sea, in memory of his son.

Name _____

Questions about
Theseus and the Minotaur
&
Daedalus and Icarus

1. What good thing did King Minos do? What bad thing?

   _____

   _____

2. How would you describe the Minotaur?

   _____

   _____

3. Why did Theseus volunteer to be one of the Athenian hostages?

   _____

   _____

4. What did Ariadne do to help Theseus?

   _____

   _____

5. What warning did Daedalus give Icarus? Why?

   _____

   _____

6. How would you change the construction of the wings to prevent the problem?

   _____

   _____

       Myths & Legends • EMC 759

Name _____

Theseus and the Minotaur
&
Daedalus and Icarus
Vocabulary

A. Write the number of each word by its meaning.

1. labyrinth   _____ a prisoner held as security

2. hostage   _____ a maze

3. architect   _____ greatly feared

4. dreaded   _____ held in confinement

5. maidens   _____ the way in

6. imprisoned   _____ a person who designs buildings

7. entrance   _____ recollection

8. memory   _____ spread wide

9. outstretched   _____ unmarried girls

B. Write a sentence about a memory you have.

_____

C. Write a sentence about something you dread.

_____

D. Describe the entrance to your home.

_____

_____

Name _____

Theseus and the Minotaur
&
Daedalus and Icarus
Figures of Speech

Similes

A **simile** compares two things using the words *like* or *as*.

1. Here is a simile from the story.

> *Daedalus, like a mother bird teaching her young, taught Icarus to fly.*

Tell the two things being compared in the simile.

_____   _____.

2. Write about an experience you have had, comparing it to an event from this myth.

Example: *When I looked at the map of trails in the park, I felt like Theseus walking into the labyrinth.*

_____

_____

_____

_____

_____

Personification

Personification gives animals, ideas, or objects human form and characteristics.

What things are personified in these two examples from this myth?

1. It swallowed his words.   _____

2. It rolled in front of him, leading the way.   _____

Theseus and the Minotaur
&
Daedalus and Icarus
Heroes and Villains

1. Do you consider Theseus a hero? Give examples from the myth to support your opinion.

_____

_____

_____

_____

_____

2. Do you consider Daedalus a hero? Give examples from the myth to support your opinion.

_____

_____

_____

_____

_____

3. Who is the villain in the story? Tell why you think so.

_____

_____

_____

_____

Theseus and the Minotaur
&
Daedalus and Icarus
A Labyrinth

Can you get to the center of the labyrinth?

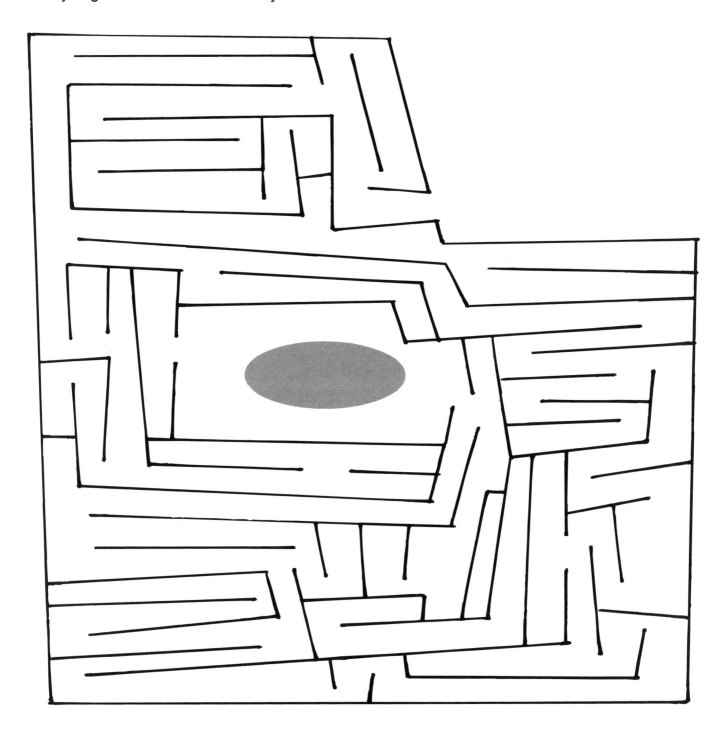

Introduction to Norse Myths

About 1000 B.C., Germanic tribes began to move into the Scandinavian countries. From there they went to what is now England, France, and other European countries. Their Viking ships took settlers to the northern islands of Iceland and Greenland. Wherever they traveled, they took their myths with them. Storytellers passed these Norse tales from one generation to the next. Written versions of the myths came from Iceland, where they were recorded about A.D. 1200. The following description comes from Icelandic stories and poems. It tells how the Norse pictured their world.

An enormous ash tree, Yggdrasil, held nine Norse worlds in place with three long roots. The worlds were divided into three levels. The tree root that held the highest level in place was cared for by the three fates—the goddesses Yesterday, Today, and Tomorrow. This highest world was the home of all the gods and goddesses. Gods who were warriors lived in Asgard. Other gods and goddesses inhabited the land of Vanaheim. The gods could descend to the middle lands on a rainbow bridge called Bifrost that was guarded by the god Heimdall.

The middle worlds were set aside for people, giants, elves, and dwarfs. People inhabited the world called Midgard. An ocean that was guarded by the serpent Jormungand surrounded these lands. His long body circled all the way around the land.

The third level was the Land of the Dead. It was covered with snow and ice that was never warmed by sunlight. The goddess Hel ruled over those who came to the lower region. The eternal fires of Muspell burned here.

The Norse gods and goddesses were like the people who worshipped them. They could be jealous and angry, and sometimes they made the wrong decisions. Unlike the Greek gods and goddesses, they could die.

Odin, the god of war, was the greatest of the gods. If someone made him angry, he sought revenge. He started wars and decided their outcome. From Valhalla, his home, Odin overlooked the nine worlds. A raven sat on each of Odin's shoulders. They flew out every day to see what was happening in the Norse kingdoms. They reported what they saw to Odin. Odin was a poet as well as a warrior, so he ruled over both Asgard and Vanaheim.

Frigg, Odin's wife, could foresee the future, but she didn't tell others what she knew. She cared for women and children.

The god Balder, who was Frigg and Odin's son, was loving and kind. He was known for his wisdom. His brother, the blind Hoder, was responsible for Balder's death.

Thor, the god of thunder, was the first son of Odin. He was powerful and very large. He protected people and the gods. Two goats pulled Thor's chariot. His famous hammer was named Mjollnir. A flash of lightning appeared when it struck the earth.

Frey was the god of the Earth and people. He was in charge of the rain and the sun. His sister, Freyja, was the goddess of love. She was the most important goddess next to Frigg.

Loki wasn't an official god, but he lived among the gods and goddesses. He had magic powers and could change into other people and animals. His mischievous ways caused problems for the gods and all who knew him. Hel, ruler of the Land of the Dead, was his daughter.

Thor and the Giants

Thor, Loki, and Thialfi, a swift runner, set out for Utgard, the Land of the Giants. When night fell, the travelers went inside a cave to sleep. All night they heard loud noises. As they left in the morning, they stumbled into a snoring giant. In the morning light, they discovered that their cave was really the giant's glove.

When Skrymir, the giant, awoke, he agreed to guide them to Utgard. He stuffed their food into his knapsack and strode off. The travelers had to run to keep him in sight. At sunset the giant stopped and told them he was too tired to eat. He gave them the bag of food and went to sleep. Neither Thor nor Loki could open the iron ties on the bag, so the travelers had no dinner.

Skrymir snored so loudly that no one else could sleep. Thor got up and swung his magic hammer at the giant's head. Skrymir sat up. "An acorn must have fallen from the tree and hit me on the head," he said. He lay back down and began to snore again.

Thor swung his hammer a second time. Skrymir yawned. "A leaf must have fallen on my nose," he said. "Thor, I see you're awake too. No one can sleep with acorns and leaves falling from the tree. It's a long journey to Utgard. Let's be on our way."

Thor couldn't believe the giant had survived his blows. The travelers walked the rest of the night and the next day. Skrymir stopped when he came to two different paths.

"I'm going to the left. If you follow the other path, you will be in Utgard before dark." The giant strode off with their food.

The travelers walked until they came to a gate that touched the clouds. It opened and they entered the giants' city. They went inside a building that was larger than any building in the land of the gods.

"Guests!" shouted a giant seated at a table. "We have few visitors. You are welcome, but you must prove your strength if you stay with us. I recognize you, Thor, but I didn't think you were so scrawny. Those stories about you killing giants must be false."

Thor raised his hammer to strike the giant, but he remembered that his blows to Skrymir's head had not harmed him.

"What can the three of you do to prove you are worthy of our company?" the giant asked.

"I am the fastest runner in Midgard," said Thialfi. "I challenge one of the giants to a race."

A long-legged giant appeared. Thialfi and the giant raced on the road that circled Utgard. The giant ran around twice before Thialfi was at the halfway mark.

"And what about you?" the leader asked Loki.

"I can eat more than any giant," said Loki, who hadn't eaten for two days.

The giant set up a wooden trough that stretched across the room. He filled it with meat. Loki started eating at one end of the trough, and a giant began eating at the other. The giant and Loki reached the middle at the same time. The giant won because he had eaten the meat, the bones, and the trough itself.

"Your friends have failed, Thor. How can you prove your strength?" the giant asked.

"I can drink more than anyone," Thor said.

The giant brought out a hollow horn and handed one end to Thor. No matter how much Thor drank, the horn stayed almost full.

"The mighty Thor isn't as great as I thought, but I'll give you another chance," said the giant. "Lift this giant cat."

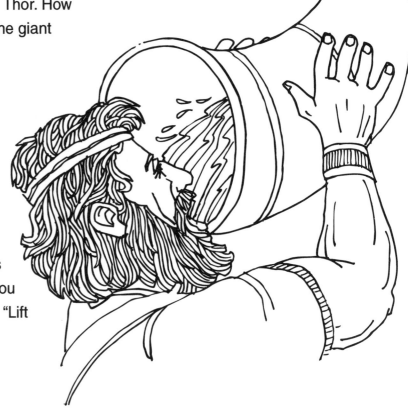

Myths & Legends • EMC 759

Thor tried to lift the animal. Only one of the animal's front feet left the ground. Humiliated, Thor gave up.

"No one at Utgard will wrestle a god as weak as you," said the giant, "but you may wrestle with my mother."

An old crone with a cane hobbled into the room. She put a hammerlock on Thor and floored him.

The giant led the defeated travelers out the gate. Thor said, "I brought shame to the gods."

"Things are not always what they seem," their host said. "I am really Skrymir, the giant from the forest. Indeed, Thor, you are mightier than any giant. When you struck at me with your hammer, I rolled to the side and you made deep valleys in the earth. Your blows would have killed me.

"The giant who ran the race was Thought, who travels faster than any runner. The one who challenged Loki was Fire, who eats wood as well as bones and meat."

"That may be true," said Thor, "but we didn't win one contest."

The giant laughed. "Your drinking horn was attached to the sea. No one can drink the sea dry. As for the cat, it was really the sea monster that circles Midgard. No god or giant can lift it. The woman you wrestled was Old Age. No one wins that contest!"

Thor turned to strike the giant with his hammer, but the giant and the city had disappeared.

Name _____

Questions about
Thor and the Giants

1. Who are the main characters in this story?

   _____

   _____

2. What did Skrymir compare Thor's hammer blows to?

   _____

   _____

3. How did Thor and his companions describe their worthiness to be in the giants' company?

   _____

   _____

   _____

4. Explain how Skrymir tricked the travelers.

   _____

   _____

   _____

   _____

5. What was the final trick?

   _____

   _____

Name _____

Thor and the Giants
Vocabulary

A. Write each word below on the line in front of its synonym.

humiliated	defeated	floored	survived	stumbled
appeared	failed	hobbled	challenged	disappeared

1. _____ remained alive

2. _____ seemed

3. _____ tripped

4. _____ embarrassed

5. _____ knocked down

6. _____ lost

7. _____ unsuccessful

8. _____ limped

9. _____ vanished

10. _____ dared

B. Write sentences using four of the words above.

_____

_____

_____

_____

Name _____

Thor and the Giants
Personification

Personification gives animals, ideas, or inanimate objects human form and characteristics. Myths and legends often have many examples of personification.

Tell how the following ideas or objects were personified in *Thor and the Giants*. Then explain what each sentence means.

Old Age _____

No one wins a contest with Old Age.

_____

_____

Thought _____

Thought travels faster than any runner.

_____

_____

Fire _____

Fire eats wood as well as bones and meat.

_____

_____

Name _____

Thor and the Giants
Giving the Reader Clues

Write a clue from the story that would enable you to make each of the following conclusions.

1. Skrymir walked fast.

_____

2. The gates to the city were very tall.

_____

3. Thor's hammer blows were powerful.

_____

● ● ● Forming an Opinion ● ● ●

Skrymir greeted Thor by saying, "I recognize you, Thor, but I didn't think you were so scrawny. Those stories about you killing giants must be false."

1. Why did Skrymir greet Thor in this way?

_____

_____

2. Do you think Skrymir really believed that Thor was scrawny or strong? Give examples from the story to support your opinion.

_____

_____

_____

_____

Thor's Hammer

Thor and his wife, Sif, lived in Asgard in the land of the gods and goddesses. Sif had long, golden hair that was the envy of all the other goddesses. One night, when Thor was away, the mischievous Loki entered Sif's room. He chopped off Sif's beautiful tresses while she slept. But Thor found out that the culprit was Loki. He threatened to destroy Loki if Sif's hair was not replaced.

Loki visited the caves of the elves who made treasures from underground metals. Loki pleaded with them to construct a head of golden hair for Sif. The elves made the hair and created other gifts to please the gods. They designed a magic ship that could hold all the Norse gods and goddesses. When the ship wasn't in use, it shrank to the size of a hand-held toy. They also forged a sword made from precious metals.

But Loki thought that it would require still more treasures to win the favor of Thor and the other gods and goddesses. He visited the elves and challenged them to make gifts finer than the boat and the sword. He foolishly promised to give the elves his head if they could make better gifts.

The elves made a glittering gold boar, a golden armband, and a jewel-handled hammer called Mjollnir. The sly Loki escaped with the treasures before the elves could cut off his head.

When Loki returned to Asgard, he gave the hammer to Thor, the hair to Sif, and the rest of the treasures to Odin and Frey. The angry elves followed Loki and demanded that the gods judge their work.

Loki argued that the boar was not as practical as a magic ship, and the handle of the hammer was not as perfect as the elves claimed. Odin and the others ruled in favor of the elves. Loki owed them his head.

"You can't take my head without taking part of my neck," Loki argued. "My neck is not part of the bargain." The elves studied Loki's neck and head. They reluctantly agreed that Loki was right. However, the elves claimed, they did own Loki's head and could do what they wished with it. To punish him, they sewed his mouth shut. It was a long time before Loki could undo the stitches and get into trouble again.

Thor put his new hammer to good use. He created lightning when he threw it to Earth, and used it to protect the gods from giants.

Since the giants couldn't win battles against Thor when he had his hammer, they decided to steal Mjollnir. While Thor napped in the forest, the giant Thrym stole the hammer and hid it underground.

Thor sent Loki to see Thrym and bargain for the hammer. "I will return Mjollnir if the goddess Freyja will be my bride," Thrym said.

Loki returned to the gods and goddesses and told them the ransom Thrym demanded for the hammer. Freyja refused to marry Thrym. Loki argued, but the gods refused to send her.

"I have another plan," Loki said. "We'll dress Thor as a bride. When Thrym gives us the hammer, Thor can destroy him with it."

When Thor realized there was no other way to get his mighty hammer back, he reluctantly agreed to wear a bride's veil and dress. Disguised as Freyja, Thor journeyed with Loki to the Land of the Giants. Thrym greeted them when they arrived at his cave.

"She is as beautiful as any goddess, I'm sure," praised Thrym, "but I had no idea she was this tall. Her boots are bigger than mine!"

"It was a long walk," Loki explained. "She wore large boots in case her feet swelled. Since you are a giant, and quite tall yourself, her size is not important."

Thrym agreed. He set out a wedding feast for the guests. Thor ate a whole ox, a basket of salmon, and washed his food down with huge bowls of mead.

"She has a giant appetite," Thrym said.

"It's a custom with goddesses," Loki explained. "The bride doesn't eat for days before her wedding. She's very hungry after such a long fast."

"I must have just one look at my bride's face," Thrym said. He lifted the veil and jumped up from the bench, almost knocking over Thor and Loki. "Those eyes! They're as red as fire."

"It's nothing," Loki said. "She hasn't slept for a week just thinking about her husband-to-be. If you give me Mjollnir, the wedding can begin."

Thrym left the room and brought back the hammer.

"Let the bride hold it for good luck," Loki said. Thrym handed the hammer to Thor.

Thor tore off the veil and struck the giant with Mjollnir. Loki and Thor fled just as the other giants arrived for the wedding. Loki turned himself into a hawk and flew away, leaving Thor and Mjollnir to fight the wedding guests. Thor felled the giants, one by one, and hurried back to Asgard to tell his tale.

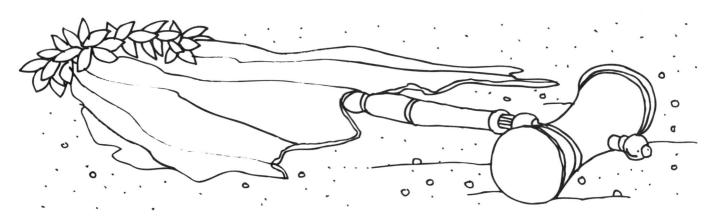

Name _____

Questions about
Thor's Hammer

. Do you think Loki was a good friend to Thor? Give examples from the story to support your ideas.

_____

_____

_____

. Explain how Thor got the hammer Mjollnir.

_____

_____

. Why did the giants steal Mjollnir?

_____

_____

. What was Loki's plan for getting Mjollnir back?

_____

_____

. What three concerns did Thrym have about his "bride"?

_____

_____

_____

Name _____

Thor's Hammer
Vocabulary

A. Write each word below on the line in front of its meaning.

mischievous	tresses	culprit	pleaded	forged
in favor of	practical	bargain	ransom	reluctantly

1. _____ payment demanded

2. _____ long locks of hair

3. _____ begged for

4. _____ unwillingly

5. _____ irresponsibly playful

6. _____ deal

7. _____ in support of

8. _____ shaped by heating and hammering

9. _____ suitable for use

10. _____ a person who committed an offense

B. Use words from the list above to complete these sentences.

1. The tennis shoes were more _____ than the satin slippers.

2. She combed her black _____.

3. The kidnapper demanded a _____.

4. The two boys made a _____.

5. The mother agreed _____.

6. The blacksmith _____ the sword.

Name _____

Thor's Hammer
Sequencing

Number the events in chronological order.

_____ Thrym stole Mjollnir.

_____ Loki cut Sif's hair.

_____ Thor tricked Thrym by pretending to be his bride.

_____ Freyja refused to marry Thrym.

_____ Loki asked the elves to create gifts for the gods.

_____ Loki made a bargain with the elves.

_____ The elves sewed Loki's mouth shut.

_____ Loki turned himself into a hawk.

_____ Thor returned to Asgard to tell his tale.

_____ Thor napped in the forest.

● ● ● Main Ideas ● ● ●

What was the most significant event in the story? Tell why you believe as you do.

_____

_____

_____

_____

Name _____

Thor's Hammer
Prefixes

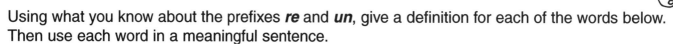

Using what you know about the prefixes *re* and *un*, give a definition for each of the words below. Then use each word in a meaningful sentence.

re = again

un = not

replace _____

_____

_____

unconscious _____

_____

_____

return _____

_____

_____

unaware _____

_____

_____

reread _____

_____

_____

uncertain _____

_____

_____

refund _____

_____

_____

unbroken _____

_____

_____

Balder the Good

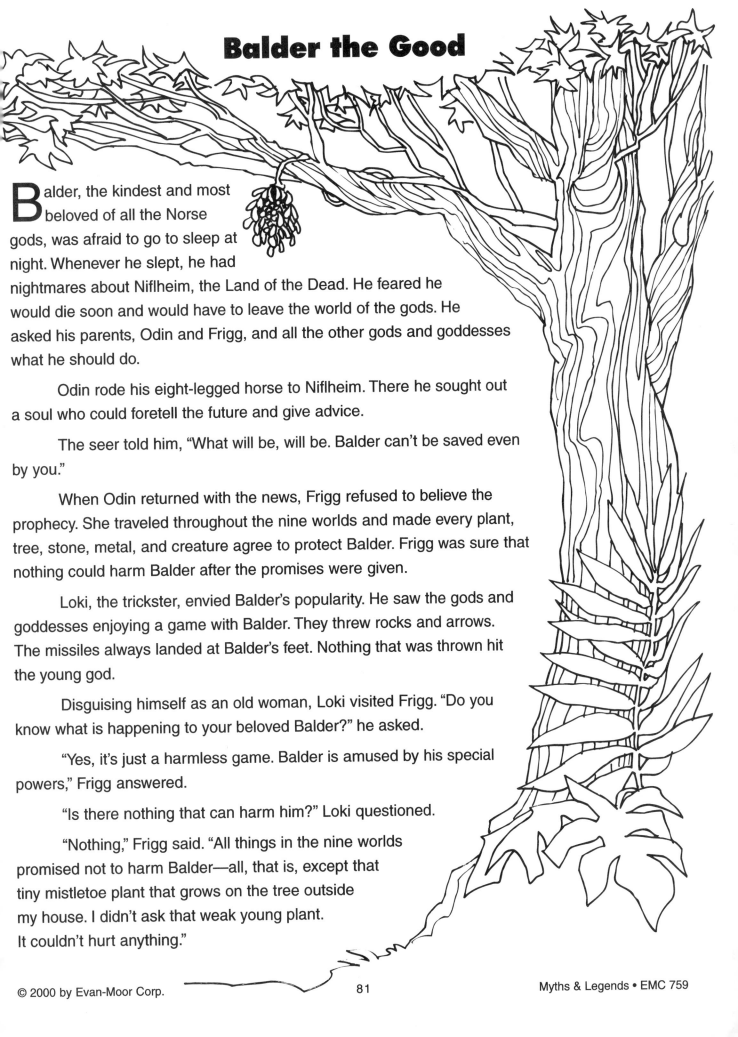

Balder, the kindest and most beloved of all the Norse gods, was afraid to go to sleep at night. Whenever he slept, he had nightmares about Niflheim, the Land of the Dead. He feared he would die soon and would have to leave the world of the gods. He asked his parents, Odin and Frigg, and all the other gods and goddesses what he should do.

Odin rode his eight-legged horse to Niflheim. There he sought out a soul who could foretell the future and give advice.

The seer told him, "What will be, will be. Balder can't be saved even by you."

When Odin returned with the news, Frigg refused to believe the prophecy. She traveled throughout the nine worlds and made every plant, tree, stone, metal, and creature agree to protect Balder. Frigg was sure that nothing could harm Balder after the promises were given.

Loki, the trickster, envied Balder's popularity. He saw the gods and goddesses enjoying a game with Balder. They threw rocks and arrows. The missiles always landed at Balder's feet. Nothing that was thrown hit the young god.

Disguising himself as an old woman, Loki visited Frigg. "Do you know what is happening to your beloved Balder?" he asked.

"Yes, it's just a harmless game. Balder is amused by his special powers," Frigg answered.

"Is there nothing that can harm him?" Loki questioned.

"Nothing," Frigg said. "All things in the nine worlds promised not to harm Balder—all, that is, except that tiny mistletoe plant that grows on the tree outside my house. I didn't ask that weak young plant. It couldn't hurt anything."

 Myths & Legends • EMC 759

"I see," answered Loki, and he left quickly.

Loki changed back into his own form. He carved a sharply pointed stick from the mistletoe plant and returned to where the game was being played. He saw Balder's brother Hoder standing alone. "Hoder," Loki said, "why aren't you taking part in the game?"

"You know I am blind," said Hoder. "I don't know which direction to throw a stone or an arrow even if I had one."

"I will help you," Loki said. He handed Hoder the pointed stick made from the mistletoe and showed him how to aim it.

Hoder threw the stick at Balder and it hit him. The point pierced Balder's heart, and the young god died.

All the gods and goddesses wept when they saw what had happened. They knew Loki was to blame, but he had escaped while all were mourning for Balder.

Frigg asked Hermod, one of Odin's sons, to go to Niflheim and talk to Hel, the Queen of the Dead. Balder's return was worth any ransom Hel could ask. Hermod assured Hel that all creatures, plants, and objects grieved for Balder. "The gods and goddesses fear the worlds will suffer without his wisdom and kindness," said Hermod.

Hel agreed to release Balder if everything in all nine worlds wept for him. "You must prove that everything loves Balder. If there is anything that refuses to weep," she said, "he will stay here with me."

Hermod assured the dreaded queen that no blade of grass or rock would remain tearless.

The gods and goddesses traveled the nine worlds. Each object, creature, and all plant life agreed to shed tears for Balder. But at last, one horrible giantess refused to shed a single tear. So Balder had to remain in Niflheim.

It was soon discovered that the giantess who refused to cry was Loki in disguise. The gods and goddesses searched everywhere for the wicked trickster and vowed to punish him.

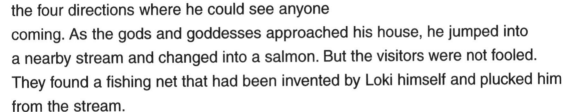

Loki hid from the gods by changing his shape whenever they were near. He fled to a mountain and built a house with a door facing each of the four directions where he could see anyone coming. As the gods and goddesses approached his house, he jumped into a nearby stream and changed into a salmon. But the visitors were not fooled. They found a fishing net that had been invented by Loki himself and plucked him from the stream.

The gods and goddesses took Loki to a cave and bound him with a tie that couldn't be broken. A poisonous serpent was positioned over his head so that its deadly venom dripped from its fangs onto Loki's face.

Loki remained in the cave until the time of Ragnarok, the end of the world, when the mountain and cave crumbled in an earthquake. Loki, Hel, and an army of dead souls joined the giants to fight the gods and goddesses. Almost all who fought were killed. Fire and flood destroyed the nine worlds.

Then, once more, land rose up from the sea. Balder returned from the dead, and life began again for the few who survived Ragnarok.

                   Myths & Legends • EMC 759

Name _____

Questions about
Balder the Good

1. What was Balder's problem?

   _____

2. What did Odin do to help Balder? What did Frigg do?

   _____

   _____

   _____

3. Who was blamed for Balder's death? Was the blame justified? Give examples to support
   your answer.

   _____

   _____

   _____

4. What bargain did Hermod make with Hel?

   _____

   _____

   _____

5. How was Loki a problem in carrying out the bargain?

   _____

   _____

   _____

84

Name _____

Balder the Good
Identifying and Analyzing Characters

Write the name of each character or event from the story on the line in front of the appropriate description.

Balder   Odin   Ragnarok

Loki   Hoder   Hel

1. _____ ruler of Niflheim

2. _____ blind brother

3. _____ Balder's father

4. _____ trickster

5. _____ beloved god

6. _____ end of the world

Classify the following characters as good or bad. Give an explanation for each classification.

Good   **Bad**

Hel   ☐   ☐   _____

_____

Balder   ☐   ☐   _____

_____

Frigg   ☐   ☐   _____

_____

Loki   ☐   ☐   _____

_____

Odin   ☐   ☐   _____

_____

Name _____

Balder the Good
Sequencing Events

A. Number the story events to show the sequence in which they occurred.

_____ Loki disguised himself as a giantess.

_____ Frigg made all things promise to protect Balder.

_____ Loki was imprisoned in a cave.

_____ Balder had nightmares.

_____ Loki tricked Hoder into killing Balder.

_____ Loki disguised himself as an old woman.

_____ Frigg tried to ransom Balder from Hel.

_____ Loki became a salmon.

_____ Balder returned.

B. Write two additional story events. Tell where each event occurs in the above sequence.

1. _____

_____

This event comes between event number _____ and event number _____.

2. _____

_____

This event comes between event number _____ and event number _____.

Name _____

Balder the Good
Vocabulary

A. Write the number of each word by its definition.

1. prophecy   _____ guaranteed

2. envied   _____ a statement that tells what will happen

3. missiles   _____ begrudged; felt jealous

4. harmless   _____ to let go

5. pierced   _____ fell apart

6. ransom   _____ penetrated

7. release   _____ safe; not a threat

8. assured   _____ a payment for the release of a captive

9. trickster   _____ a person who deceives people

10. crumbled   _____ objects for throwing

B. Use words from the list above to complete these sentences.

1. Hermod _____ Hel that all grieved for Balder.

2. The sharp stick _____ Balder's heart.

3. Loki _____ Balder's popularity.

4. The gods said that nothing could stop the _____ from coming true.

C. On another sheet of paper, write about something you consider harmless.

              Myths & Legends • EMC 759

Introduction to a World of Myths

Gilgamesh and Enkidu, a legend from the Middle East

One of the earliest recorded legends is the story of Gilgamesh, a hero king. The stories come from Mesopotamia and were written on clay tablets between 2100 and 600 B.C. The goddess Nintu was Gilgamesh's mother. His father was a mortal king. Two deities mentioned in the legend are Ishtar, the goddess of love and war, and Shamash, the god of the sun.

Maui and the Sun, a Hawaiian myth

The Polynesian people worshipped the gods of nature. *Maui and the Sun* explains why days are long in summer and short in winter. Maui was a trickster, both mortal and god, who sometimes helped people and often got in trouble.

The Earth and Sky, an African myth from Benin

The people in Benin believed that different gods controlled nature. Rain was necessary to grow their food, but sometimes the gods held it back and there was drought. In this myth, an angry god holds back the rain until his brother agrees to share the Earth.

The Ten Suns, a Chinese myth

At one time there were ten suns in the sky causing the Earth to burn. *The Ten Suns* explains why there is just one sun now.

How It All Began, a Quiche Mayan myth from Guatemala

How It All Began comes from the Popul Vuh, a Mayan book that was written in Spanish in the middle of the sixteenth century. In this story, the Creator, after several failures, successfully breathes life into beings who can pray to the gods.

Sedna, Goddess of the Sea, an Inuit myth from the Arctic

The Inuit people live in the Arctic. This myth explains how Sedna, the mother of the seals and whales, became the goddess of the sea.

The Sky Woman, an Onondaga myth

The Onondaga people are one of the Iroquois Nations. *The Sky Woman* tells how the Earth was formed on a turtle's back. Other Native American people in the northeastern part of Canada and the United States tell different versions of this myth.

Gilgamesh and Enkidu

A Middle East Legend

Long ago, the youthful King Gilgamesh ruled over the land of Uruk. He was part god and part mortal. He was known as a great builder, and he always had a new project for his subjects to finish. Day after day he commanded his people to build walls, buildings, and temples. The overworked people tired of the tasks Gilgamesh demanded.

Gilgamesh was a great warrior as well as a builder. He liked nothing better than one-on-one battles with the young men in his kingdom. Gilgamesh was very strong and he always won.

The people of Uruk complained to the gods about the work and fighting they had to do for Gilgamesh. "Our king doesn't honor traditions," they said. "He does whatever he wishes."

The Earth goddess agreed. From a lump of clay, she created a man named Enkidu, who was the equal of Gilgamesh. "This man will be a companion for Gilgamesh and help him rule wisely," she said.

Enkidu was wild. He was as hairy as the beasts, ate grass like the animals, and had no knowledge of people.

A hunter from Uruk set traps in the grasslands where Enkidu lived. The next day, when the hunter returned to collect the animals caught in the traps, he found his traps destroyed. When the hunter walked near the water hole, he saw Enkidu drinking with the animals. As the hunter aimed his arrow at a gazelle, Enkidu yelled and charged. All the animals fled. The hunter, fearing for his life, ran also.

The hunter went to King Gilgamesh and told him about the wild man. "He is as strong as you are, my king."

"I must see this man and fight against him. This time, I will fight with one who is my equal. I will send a priestess from Goddess Ishtar's temple to teach him how to be human. She can then bring him to Uruk."

When the priestess found Enkidu, she said, "You are not like these animals. I will sing songs to you about life and tell you how to live like the people of Uruk."

When the priestess finished her songs and stories, Enkidu returned to the water hole to say good-bye to his friends the animals. They fled from him, knowing that he was no longer one of them. He was human and they feared him.

Enkidu followed the priestess to Uruk. Gilgamesh was waiting for him by the city gate. He pushed Enkidu aside and would not let him enter the city. The two men fought. Enkidu knew he was stronger than Gilgamesh, but he didn't wish to injure the king. "I can't defeat you," Enkidu said as the two men struggled. The fighting ended, and Enkidu went to the palace with Gilgamesh.

All the people of Uruk welcomed Enkidu. Now Gilgamesh had someone his equal to battle. The king's adventures with Enkidu kept him busy. He didn't have time to give the people new projects. He followed all traditions so that Enkidu could learn about them.

Gilgamesh wanted to accomplish great deeds so people would remember him after his death. He talked Enkidu into a trip to the Cedar Mountains to gather the strong, sweet-smelling wood. "I will challenge Humbaba, the monster who guards the trees," Gilgamesh said. "If I destroy this evil creature, my name will be recorded and remembered forever."

Enkidu, Gilgamesh, and soldiers from Uruk set out on the long journey. After several days they came to the towering cedar trees. Gilgamesh swung his ax at the tallest tree and began to chop it down.

Humbaba heard the noise and roared in anger. "Who dares to cut down my trees?" The sound of his voice made Gilgamesh tremble.

"Shamash, the god of the sun, will protect you," Enkidu said. His words gave Gilgamesh courage.

"I am Gilgamesh!" the king shouted. "I have come to rid this land of the evil Humbaba."

Together Enkidu and Gilgamesh fought Humbaba and killed him.

Not only was Gilgamesh strong, he was also very handsome. The goddess Ishtar fell in love with him and asked him to marry her. Gilgamesh refused,s even though she promised great riches and power. "You have destroyed all men who have loved you," he said.

Ishtar asked her father for the Bull of Heaven to destroy Gilgamesh. When she sent the Bull to Uruk, his roars cracked the earth. People fell into the chasms and died.

Enkidu seized the Bull of Heaven and fought against it. He and Gilgamesh killed the bull after a long struggle. Then Enkidu insulted Ishtar and threatened her. He spoke ill words about the other deities as well. The gods and goddesses decreed that Enkidu must be punished for his deeds and his words. An illness was sent to Enkidu and he died.

Gilgamesh grieved for his friend and gave Enkidu a funeral and burial worthy of a god. The people mourned Enkidu because he had tamed the wild King Gilgamesh and given him wisdom.

Name _____

Questions about
Gilgamesh and Enkidu

1. Were Gilgamesh and Enkidu friends? Justify your opinion.

_____

_____

_____

_____

2. What were Gilgamesh's strengths and weaknesses?

_____

_____

3. Why was Enkidu punished?

_____

_____

4. What was Enkidu's punishment? Do you think it was deserved? Explain why or why not.

_____

_____

_____

5. Why did Gilgamesh want to do great deeds?

_____

_____

_____

Name _____

Gilgamesh and Enkidu
Looking at Characters

1. Write a letter on the line to correctly match each story character with an action.

      a. Earth goddess   _____ cracked the earth with his roars

      b. Enkidu   _____ destroyed the hunter's traps

      c. Gilgamesh   _____ guarded the cedar trees

      d. Humbaba   _____ created a man from a lump of clay

      e. Ishtar   _____ asked Gilgamesh to marry her

      f. Bull of Heaven   _____ enjoyed fighting with Enkidu

2. Describe Gilgamesh before he met Enkidu.

  ·

_____

_____

_____

3. Describe Gilgamesh after he met Enkidu.

_____

_____

_____

4. Write a sentence that compares the two different personalities of Gilgamesh and summarizes the changes.

_____

_____

                                        Myths & Legends • EMC 759

Name _____

Gilgamesh and Enkidu
Vocabulary

A. Write the number of each word by its synonym.

1. gazelle   _____ powerful

2. destroy   _____ graceful antelope

3. stacked   _____ untamed

4. promised   _____ vowed

5. wild   _____ piled

6. strong   _____ wisdom

7. knowledge   _____ demolish

8. found   _____ young

9. overworked   _____ located

10. youthful   _____ exciting experiences

11. adventures   _____ exhausted

12. evil   _____ wicked

B. Use words from the list above to complete these sentences.

1. The hunter aimed his arrow at the _____.

2. The soldiers _____ wood from the cedar trees.

3. The _____ people were tired of Gilgamesh's demands.

4. The king's _____ with Enkidu kept him busy.

Name _____

Gilgamesh and Enkidu
Critical Thinking

Read the statements. Do you agree or disagree? Write a paragraph to express your opinions.

Enkidu was a good friend to Gilgamesh.

_____

_____

_____

_____

Gilgamesh was insensitive and used the people around him to get what he wanted.

_____

_____

_____

_____

Gilgamesh should have married Ishtar.

_____

_____

_____

_____

Maui and the Sun

A Hawaiian Myth

The sun god raced across the sky each day. He traveled so fast that people didn't have time to finish their work in the daylight. They couldn't grow enough food because there wasn't the right amount of warm sun. They were always hungry and ill-tempered.

Maui's mother, Hina-of-the-Fire, complained because the days were too short. Besides cleaning and cooking, she made tapa cloth from the bark of mulberry trees. It took months to make the cloth because she could work only when the sun was in the sky. She had to soak the bark and pound it into thin cloth. Then she pasted the strips of bark together. The tapa cloth had to dry before she could make sleeping mats and clothing.

People prayed to the sun god and asked him to slow down. But the sun moved so fast, he didn't have time to answer.

"Why does the sun hurry?" asked Maui. "He should take his time and enjoy the beauty of the Earth."

"And why do fish live in the sea?" asked Hina-of-the Fire. "It's because they've always lived there. It will always be that way. It's the same with the sun. He travels fast because he always has. He won't change. He will do what pleases him."

"I will capture him and make him move more slowly," Maui said. "Then everyone will be much happier."

"How will you capture the sun? If you go that close, the sun will burn you. No one can change the sun god's ways."

"I must try," said Maui.

Maui walked up the slope of a bubbling volcano and looked toward the east where the sun rose out of the water each morning. He waited until the sun god climbed overhead.

"Can you walk slowly today, Great Sun, so the fishermen can repair their nets before they go out to sea?" Maui asked.

The sun let off a fiery glow and hurried on his way without answering.

"What can I do?" Maui asked his mother. "The sun didn't listen when I asked politely."

"I don't know how to change the sun. Go to your grandmother— the one who prepares breakfast for the sun god. She sets out an offering of fruit for him each morning. Maybe she will know what to do."

Maui went to his grandmother's house. "Venerable Grandmother, I've come to ask you to help me capture the sun. He moves so quickly, there isn't enough daylights. People can't finish their work."

"No man or god has been able to slow the sun. Why do you think you are worthy of this task?" his grandmother asked.

To show her how clever he was, Maui drew a rainbow across the sky. He brought rain and lightning. Birds flew through the air and sang his praises.

"If you can change the sky, you might be able to change the sun," Maui's grandmother said. "Listen carefully. Ask Hina-of-the-Sea for some of her hair, and gather plant fibers. Twist the hair and fibers together to make a strong net."

After Maui prepared the net, Maui's grandmother showed him how to set a trap for the rays of the sun. She helped him tie the net to the roots of a giant tree. Then she handed him a magic ax to use as a weapon. Maui hid near the place where the sun came for breakfast.

When the first ray of the sun reached for the fruit, it became trapped in the net. As each ray climbed out of the sea, it was entangled. Maui closed the net when the sun was caught inside it.

The sun struggled to free himself. "Who dares to stop the sun?" he bellowed. "I am the greatest god of earth and sky!"

"I am Maui. You have behaved badly. You don't listen to the people. You must move slowly so the day is as long as night. Then people will have time to finish their work before dark."

The sun scorched Maui and tried to burn everything around him. "Let me go, or I will burn whatever is in my way!"

Maui beat the sun with the magic ax his grandmother had given him. The sun cried out, "Stop! You are hurting me. I will do what you ask, but if I travel slowly every day, I won't have enough time to rest."

"Would you agree to go slowly one-half of the year and travel at your own speed the rest of the time?" Maui asked. "That way the people will have what they want and so will you."

The sun agreed to the bargain. Now there are long days in the summer so people have time to finish their work and plants have time to grow. In the winter there are long nights so there is more time to rest.

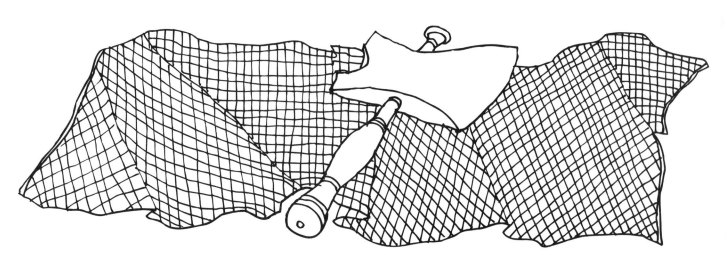

Name _____

Questions about
Maui and the Sun

1. What was the problem in this myth?

_____

_____

_____

2. How does Hina-of-the-Fire explain the problem?

_____

_____

_____

3. Why did Maui's grandmother think he could change the sun?

_____

4. How did Maui catch the sun?

_____

5. What agreement did the sun and Maui make?

_____

6. What phenomenon does this myth explain?

_____

_____

_____

Name _____

Maui and the Sun
Personification

1. In this myth the sun is personified as being rude. Give three examples that support this description.

   a. _____

   _____

   _____

   b. _____

   _____

   _____

   c. _____

   _____

   _____

2. Give two other examples of the sun's personification in this myth.

   _____

   _____

   _____

   _____

Maui and the Sun

Understanding Phrases and Words

Copy the sentence from the myth in which the following phrases and words were used. In each box write a word or phrase that has about the same meaning.

1. behaved badly

2. complained

3. entangled

4. sets out

5. clever

6. ill-tempered

Name _____

Maui and the Sun
Character Analysis

In many myths the heroes get their way through force. There are often wars and killing involved. Maui is a different type of hero. Circle the words below that could be used to describe his style of leadership. (You may need to use a dictionary.)

negotiator	willing to ask for advice	heavy-handed	contemplative
weak	dictatorial	popular	determined
polite	cruel	thoughtful	self-serving

Write a paragraph describing Maui. Tell whether or not you like his style of leadership. Justify your ideas.

_____

_____

_____

_____

_____

_____

_____

_____

_____

The Earth and Sky

An African Myth from Benin

Sagbata and Sogbo, the sons of the goddess Mawu, shared the task of ruling the world and the heavens. Unfortunately, the two brothers could not agree on anything, not even the color of the clouds.

Mawu would not take one side of the argument or the other. "You have to learn to get along," she said.

Sagbata, the older brother, packed up all their treasures. "I can't remain in the sky with you any longer. You won't listen to anything I say. Since I am the older brother, all treasures belong to me. I'm taking them to Earth. I leave water and fire here with you because I have no way to carry them."

"The sooner you go, the better," Sogbo said.

After Sagbata left, Sogbo became the favorite of his mother and the other deities. They allowed him to do whatever pleased him. To get even with his brother, who was caring for the Earth, Sogbo kept the rain in the sky and would not allow any water to fall on the Earth.

The plants didn't grow, and the people and animals were hungry. The people went to Sagbata and complained. "Why should we worship you when the Earth burns and there is no water? Go back to the sky. We lived well before you descended to Earth. You bring us misfortune."

Myths & Legends • EMC 759

"The rains will come," Sagbata said. Weeks, months, and years passed. It didn't rain.

Sagbata called two sky prophets to him and asked them why it didn't rain. "Your brother is holding back the rain. Until you can live peacefully, the rain will stay in the sky," they told him.

"I can't climb back to the sky to talk to my brother. It's too far. What can I do?"

"Call the wututu bird and ask him to take a message to your brother. If you offer to share the Earth, he might share the rain," the sky prophets said.

The wututu bird answered Sagbata's call. "Take this message to my brother," requested Sagbata. "Tell him that I have been selfish. I will let him rule the Earth with me. He can care for the villages and all the people."

The wututu bird flew back to the land of the sky and delivered the message to Sogbo. "Tell Sagbata that I will agree to help him rule the Earth," replied Sogbo.

The wututu bird flew back to Earth. Before he had returned to Sagbata, it began to rain. Sagbata greeted the bird and said, "I know my brother has accepted my offer. Because you have served the two of us well, I will tell all people on Earth that you are sacred and cannot be harmed."

The two brothers became good friends. The wututu bird carried messages of goodwill from one brother to the other. The grass and plants grew again, and the people weren't hungry anymore.

Name _____

Questions about
The Earth and Sky

. What is the initial problem in this myth?

_____

. How did Mawu deal with her arguing sons?

_____

_____

. Did Sagbata's exit from the sky solve the problem? Tell why or why not.

_____

_____

. What lesson could be learned from this myth?

_____

_____

. Do you think Mawu was right in the way she dealt with her sons? Explain why you think as
  you do.

_____

_____

_____

Name _____

The Earth and Sky
Vocabulary

The Earth and Sky is a myth about revenge and reconciliation.

Define *revenge*.

_____

_____

Give an example of revenge in the story.

_____

_____

_____

Define *reconciliation*.

_____

_____

Give an example of reconciliation in the story.

_____

_____

_____

Give examples of revenge and reconciliation that you have heard about in your community or in the world at large.

_____

_____

_____

_____

_____

_____

Name _____

The Earth and Sky
Prefixes

Draw a line to match each prefix with its meaning.

de	not
mis	do the opposite of
un	badly or wrongly
re	back or again

Use each word below in a sentence. For each word, write a word or phrase that has a similar meaning and a word or phrase that has an opposite meaning.

1. **descend**

_____

_____   _____
        same   opposite

2. **misfortune**

_____

_____   _____
        same   opposite

3. **unwise**

_____

_____   _____
        same   opposite

4. **return**

_____

_____   _____
        same   opposite

The Earth and Sky
Writing a Description

The wututu bird served Sagbata as an emissary to his brother. The myth doesn't describe the wututu bird. All the reader knows is that the bird is capable of going a long way and relaying a message.

Think about what the wututu bird might look like. How might it move and sound? Write an interesting description of the bird.

_____

_____

_____

_____

_____

_____

_____

_____

_____

_____

The Ten Suns

A Chinese Myth

Long ago there were ten suns, not one. Their mother was married to Di Jun, who was the god of the east. The sun children were well cared for. Each night their mother bathed them in a warm pool and took them to a giant mulberry tree. The suns had the bodies of birds, and they perched in the tree until it was time for them to make the next day's journey across the sky.

After the night had passed, their mother hitched a team of dragons to a golden chariot. She selected one of the suns to drive the chariot. There were ten days in a week at that time, so each sun traveled across the sky once each week. People on Earth had no idea there were so many suns. They went about their work, enjoying warm, sunny days.

The ten suns became bored. Every day was the same. Their mother made all the decisions for them. The drive across the sky was very lonely. The only fun they had was chattering together in the tree or throwing berries at each other when their mother wasn't watching.

One morning all ten suns climbed into the chariot. Their mother tried to stop them, but they wouldn't listen. "Come back!" she called as they rode into the sky. "Your father, Di Jun, will be angry."

The suns drove higher. When the suns traveled together, their flames filled the sky. They scorched the Earth and trees burned. Rivers and lakes dried. All the fish and other creatures that lived in the water died. The beasts in the forest were thirsty, and there was no water to drink. People and animals on farms died from the heat.

Myths & Legends • EMC 759

Day after day, the ten suns rode together across the sky. They laughed and sang and teased the dragons that pulled their chariot. They didn't worry about the Earth.

Their mother went to Di Jun and said, "What can I do? The children won't listen to me. Each day, they all climb into the chariot together. They are burning the Earth. Perhaps they will listen to you."

The people prayed to Di Jun. "Deliver us from the heat your children send to Earth. The ground is cracked and burnt. There is no food left for us or for the animals. Speak to them, or soon you will have no people to rule."

Di Jun went to the tree that night and told the suns that they couldn't cross the sky together. "You are destroying the Earth. There is no water left. Your mother and the people have asked me to stop you from riding together."

The suns, perched in the tree, chirped noisily.

Di Jun, thinking the suns had agreed to obey him, returned to his palace. He assured his wife and the people on Earth that the suns had given their word. "They have promised to ride across the sky one at a time."

At dawn the next day, all the suns climbed back into the chariot. Their mother tried to pull them out and put them back in the tree. Whenever she took one out, another climbed back in.

Their mother ran back to Di Jun and told him what had happened. By the time he reached the mulberry tree, the chariot was already in the sky. The clouds dried when the chariot came near them, and there were so many fires burning on Earth that the smoke turned the sky as black as the night sky.

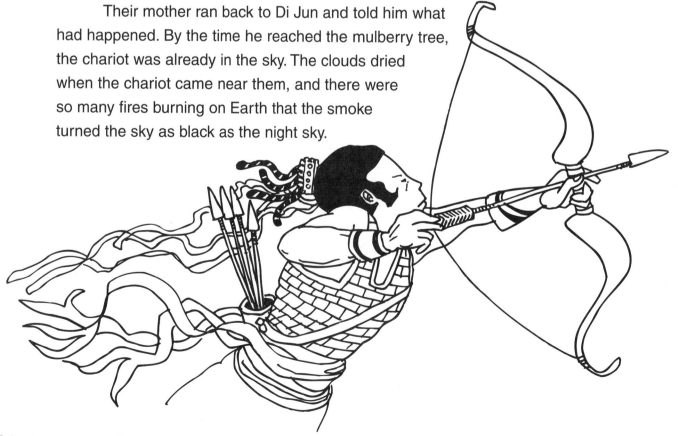

Myths & Legends • EMC 759

The people went to the emperor and asked for his help. "There will be nothing left for you to rule if you don't stop the ten suns," they said.

The emperor called for his council. They discussed the problem until the suns were directly over the palace. The gold on the walls began to melt.

The emperor realized that there was no time for talk. He sent the council home and called for the royal archer.

The archer was a giant, and he could shoot an arrow so high that it never returned to Earth.

"You must shoot the ten suns before the Earth dies," the emperor said.

The archer filled a quiver with ten arrows and selected an enormous golden bow. He climbed to the top of a mountain and readied his bow as the suns' chariot came closer. He aimed the first nine arrows carefully, and each one hit its mark. The wounded suns fell from the chariot in the form of birds. Their golden feathers floated in the air.

When there was one sun left in the chariot, the archer fit the last arrow in the bow. He felt someone tugging at his arm.

"Wait," said a voice. "Don't shoot the last sun from the sky." The archer turned and saw the suns' mother. "If there is no sun left in the sky, it will be worse than too many. Without sunlight, plants won't grow. There will be nothing to eat. Save one of my children."

The archer nodded and he handed the suns' mother the last arrow.

From that time, there has been just one sun in the sky.

Name _____

Questions about
The Ten Suns

1. Describe the sun children. Tell how they looked and what they did.

_____

_____

_____

_____

2. Tell what problem developed when the suns became bored.

_____

_____

_____

3. What caused the emperor to act quickly?

_____

_____

_____

4. Why did the archer save one sun?

_____

_____

_____

     Myths & Legends • EMC 759

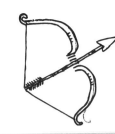

The Ten Suns
Character Analysis

Describe the mother in the myth. Would you consider the suns' mother a good mother? Justify your opinion.

_____

_____

_____

_____

_____

Describe the father as portrayed by Di Jun. Would you consider Di Jun a good father? Justify your opinion.

_____

_____

_____

_____

_____

Name _____

The Ten Suns
Verb Choice

The ten sun children in this myth perch, chirp, and chatter. The verbs that are used support the description of the children as "birds."

A. Write the verbs from the Word Box under the animal they best fit.

elephant

_____

_____

_____

_____

lion

_____

_____

_____

_____

Word Box	
tease	splash
plod	hunt
roar	hang
trumpet	flee
stalk	graze
swing	scramble
leap	

antelope

_____

_____

_____

monkey

_____

_____

_____

B. Describe a natural phenomenon (such as thunder, rain, wind, night) by comparing it with one of the animals. Be sure to choose verbs that support the description.

_____

_____

_____

_____

 Myths & Legends • EMC 759

Name _____

The Ten Suns

Nouns and Verbs

Many words can be used both as nouns and verbs. Use each of the words below in two sentences. In one sentence the word should be used as a noun. In the second sentence the word should be used as a verb.

quiver

noun– _____

verb– _____

fire

noun– _____

verb– _____

talk

noun– _____

verb– _____

aim

noun– _____

verb– _____

hand

noun– _____

verb– _____

　　　115　　　Myths & Legends • EMC 759

How It All Began

A Quiche Mayan Myth from Guatemala

At the beginning of time, the Creator, who was the mother and father of everything that existed, looked around. Within the four corners and four sides of the universe, there were no people or animals to praise him. No birds, fish, crabs, trees, rocks, holes, canyons, straw, or reeds could be found. There was nothing. No noise could be heard in the sky. The sea floated through space. It, too, was calm and lifeless.

The Creator set to work to fill the great void. First the Earth appeared. It was formed from the dust and mists that swirled through the universe. There were plains, mountains, canyons, and rivers. Then came the deer, birds, snakes, and other animals. They were given homes on Earth. The birds were told to live in the trees and reeds and were taught how to fly. The Creator showed some animals how to walk on four feet, and other creatures, like the snake, how to crawl on the ground.

Each kind of animal was to make its own noise. The animals were told to praise the Creator and the gods with their special voices. They squawked, roared, chirped, and squeaked, but they could not sing praises to the One who gave them life. The Creator was displeased. Clearly, the world needed another creature. It was decided that these animals would not be destroyed. Instead, they would serve as food for others.

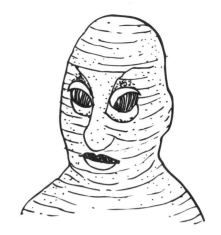

The Creator talked with the gods who had great vision and asked them to solve the problem. First, it was decided to shape people from the muddy Earth. These new creatures turned out too soft. They couldn't bathe because they dissolved in water. They made noise, but they could not think. Clearly these creatures would not serve the gods well. They were destroyed.

The next people were carved from wood. They were much hardier. They will be perfect, the Creator thought. He soon realized that there was something wrong. The wood people were unfeeling and not very smart. Their bodies were dry, without moisture or blood. The expressions on their faces never changed. They couldn't smile or cry. When the Creator told them to praise the ones who brought them life, their words had no meaning.

The wood people had many children. Their children were just like them, and none of them could praise the gods either. Clearly, these people would not do. So the Creator made sap flow from the trees. The sap ran like a river over the wood people and knocked them over. The animals broke them into pieces. The chickens pecked them because the wood people had never fed them. The dogs chewed on them because the wood people had beaten them. The grinding stones beat the wood people because they had been made to work all day and never given time to rest. Even the jars and cooking pots stomped on the wood people because their masters had left them in the fire too long and burned them.

Myths & Legends • EMC 759

The few wood people that survived climbed to the roofs of their houses for safety. The roofs collapsed. They tried to hide in caves, but the caves wouldn't let them enter. When they climbed trees, the limbs threw them back onto the ground. These wood people turned into monkeys. That is why monkeys look very much like people.

Once more the Creator decided to create people who would worship the gods. He listened to the advice of the animals. The magpie, the coyote, the crow, and the jaguar found yellow and white ears of corn growing in the fields. Food and drink were made from the corn. People were created from the food. The corn drinks made the people strong and healthy.

These corn people were our ancestors. There were four men and four women. They had many children. The corn people could speak, and their words had meaning. With their vision, they could see the whole Earth and universe. They were grateful and they gave thanks to the gods and the Creator for the Earth and sky.

The corn people prayed so well that the gods became worried. The corn people were too perfect. They saw and knew everything. They were exactly like the gods. The Creator fogged the eyes of the corn people so they saw less and didn't know everything.

All this time, there was no light in the sky—no sun, no moon, or stars. The corn people prayed for light. The Creator heard them and gave the world light so all could see what had been created. During the day, the sun warmed the Earth, the animals, and the corn people. At night the stars and moon shone in the heavens.

There was great joy when the sun rose in the mornings. All the people and creatures praised the work of the Creator and the gods. People danced and burned a sweet incense that pleased the gods. They made offerings. The world was as it should be. Clearly, it was perfect.

Name _____

Questions about
How It All Began

Describe the universe at the beginning of time.

_____

_____

Why did the Creator need to create another creature besides the animals?

_____

_____

Tell what was wrong with each of the following creatures. When the Creator realized that each creature had a problem, he did something to correct that problem. Tell what it was in each case.

a. **Creatures shaped from mud**

Problem: _____

How corrected: _____

b. **Creatures carved from wood**

Problem: _____

_____

How corrected: _____

_____

c. **Creatures created from corn food and drink**

Problem: _____

How corrected: _____

Name _____

How It All Began

Sequencing Story Events

Number the events to show the order in which they occurred.

_____ The people prayed for light.

_____ The sea floated through space.

_____ Four men and four women were created from corn.

_____ The Creator formed the Earth from dust and mist.

_____ Chickens pecked the wood people and dogs chewed on them.

_____ Creatures were shaped from muddy earth.

_____ The world was as it should be.

_____ Animals squawked, roared, chirped, and squeaked but failed to praise the Creator.

_____ The Earth appeared.

_____ Animals of all kinds were created.

Name _____

How It All Began
Remembering Details

Write each description below under the name of the group it describes.

unfeeling   turned into monkeys

dissolved in water   ancestors of human race

expressions never changed   first people created

strong and healthy   made noise, but couldn't think

too soft   their words had no meaning

too perfect

Mud People	**Wood People**	**Corn People**
_____	_____	_____
_____	_____	_____
_____	_____	_____
_____	_____	_____

Use the phrases above to write a description of each type of people created.

Mud People _____

_____

Wood People _____

_____

Corn People _____

_____

Name _____

How It All Began
Vocabulary

A. Write each word below on the line in front of its meaning.

void	expression	ancestors	grateful
perfect	incense	lifeless	collapsed

1. _____ fell down

2. _____ thankful

3. _____ relatives who have come before

4. _____ lacking vitality

5. _____ empty

6. _____ a look that tells one's feelings

7. _____ faultless

8. _____ a substance that produces a sweet smell when burned

B. Use words from the list above to complete these sentences.

1. The Mayan people believed that the corn people were their _____.

2. The _____ on the face of a wood person never changed.

3. The Creator decided to fill the _____.

4. The roofs _____ when the wooden people climbed on them.

5. The corn people were _____ and gave thanks.

Sedna, Goddess of the Sea

An Inuit Myth from the Arctic

Sedna lived with her father in the land of ice and snow. Their tent was near the sea. Most of the year, a cold, bitter wind swept across the frozen water and ground. Sedna and her father went hungry when it was too cold to fish.

There were two months in the summer when the ice melted. During that time, men from nearby settlements would paddle their kayaks to Sedna's house and ask to marry her. She refused them all—young, old, short, and tall. She felt none of them were good enough for her. "I will wait for someone who is rich, handsome, and very generous," she said.

One day a seabird stopped to rest near Sedna's house. He watched her as she sewed a fur parka. "She is more beautiful than any bird I have seen," he whispered to the wind. "I will ask her to marry me."

The bird flew back across the water to his home. He changed his form into a man and made a kayak. He returned to Sedna's house and called to her from the water, "Sedna, come with me to a warmer land. You won't need to work, and you'll sleep in a warm bearskin bed in my fur tent. I am a great hunter, and you'll never be hungry again. My friends the birds will see that you have everything you need."

Sedna could see this man was different from the others. He wore a white and gray cloak. His beaklike nose made him seem more handsome than any of her other suitors. A warm house and bed, lots of food, and a handsome husband were what she wanted.

"Daughter, don't be hasty," warned her father. "What do you know about this man? You would be better off as the wife of an Inuit hunter. Stay here with me."

 Myths & Legends • EMC 759

Sedna didn't listen. She left with the handsome stranger. They paddled to a distant, rocky island. There the winds blew as fiercely as they had around her old home. The fur tent she was promised was a smelly house made of fish skins. There were cracks and holes everywhere. The bed was a hard mat covered with damp feathers. Her handsome husband changed back into a bird.

All day long the birds fought over each scrap of raw fish. They screeched and pecked at Sedna when she took a piece for herself.

"Be content with your new home," her husband said, "and groom my handsome feathers."

Sedna wished she had listened to her father. "If he knew how I suffer," she thought, "I know he would come for me."

The following summer, Sedna's father paddled his kayak in the direction Sedna had gone. He found her on the rocky island.

"Father," she called, "take me away from here!"

Sedna's father pulled his kayak out of the water and went with her to her tent. She bundled up her parka and bone needles. The birds had stolen most of her clothes. Her only pair of boots served as warm nests.

Sedna and her father hurried to the kayak. Before they reached the water, Sedna's husband swooped down on them. He beat her father with his wings and pecked at him. Sedna's father killed the seabird with his hunting knife. Then he and Sedna paddled out to sea.

In the middle of the water, the wind and waves rocked their boat. Birds screeched overhead and threatened them. With the power of their wings, they created a stormy sea.

     Myths & Legends • EMC 759

"The birds are angry because you killed my husband," said Sedna. "What can we do?"

"If they think I have thrown you into the water to drown, they will fly away. I will rescue you later," said her father.

Sedna begged her father to let her stay in the kayak, but he threw her into the icy water and paddled away. "See!" he yelled. "I have sent Sedna to her death. Leave me in peace, and I will return to my home."

The seabirds continued to circle. Sedna grabbed the side of the kayak, tipping it to one side.

"Let go!" said her father. He pushed her fingers away. The ends of her fingers fell off and swam away as whales.

Once more, Sedna grabbed the kayak. Her father shoved her fingers into the water. The rest of her fingers fell off and became seals. Sedna drifted down into the sea.

The birds thought Sedna had drowned, and they flew back to their island. Sedna's father pulled Sedna into the boat. When they arrived home, she jumped back into the water and became the goddess of the sea. She lived there with her children, the seals and whales.

When Sedna was displeased with the hunters, she told the sea animals to hide, and the people went hungry. Each time the animals disappeared, the shaman sent his spirit to comb the tangles from Sedna's hair. This pleased her since she didn't have any fingers to hold a comb. When the shaman's spirit assured Sedna that the people would be respectful, she let the whales and seals return.

Myths & Legends • EMC 759

Name _____

Questions about
Sedna, Goddess of the Sea

1. What was Sedna looking for in a husband?

_____

_____

2. How did the seabird get Sedna to accept his proposal?

_____

_____

_____

3. Summarize Sedna's father's rescue of her.

_____

_____

_____

_____

4. What phenomenon of nature is explained by this myth?

_____

_____

_____

_____

© 2000 by Evan-Moor Corp.   126   Myths & Legends • EMC 759

Name _____

Sedna, Goddess of the Sea
Character Analysis

A. Circle the characteristics that describe Sedna.

Underline the characteristics that describe the seabird.

Draw a square around the characteristics that describe Sedna's father.

hard to please	considers self better than others	artist of disguise
jealous	deceitful	easily convinced
fingerless	wise	skeptical
careful	beautiful	

B. Write a brief description of Sedna.

_____

_____

_____

_____

Name _____

Sedna, Goddess of the Sea
Vocabulary

A. Write the number of each word by its definition.

1. kayak   _____ quick-acting

2. hasty   _____ a religious leader

3. parka   _____ a sealskin canoe

4. shaman   _____ unsatisfied

5. assured   _____ showing consideration

6. respectful   _____ promised

7. swoop   _____ a hooded coat

8. displeased   _____ to make a sudden attack

B. Use each of the following words in sentences as the designated part of speech.
 Use a dictionary if you need help.

1. **groom**

noun– _____

verb– _____

2. **bone**

noun– _____

adjective– _____

verb– _____

Name _____

Sedna, Goddess of the Sea
Recalling Story Details

Tell four promises the birdman made to Sedna. Tell what came of each promise.

Promise 1 _____

_____

_____

_____

Promise 2 _____

_____

_____

_____

Promise 3 _____

_____

_____

_____

Promise 4 _____

_____

_____

_____

The Sky Woman

An Onondaga Myth

In the beginning, there were two worlds separated by a veil of darkness. Water covered the Earth in the lower world. The only creatures who lived there were birds with webbed feet and water animals. There was no earth where they could rest. The water was their home.

The sky people lived in the upper world. They were ruled by a great chief. An enormous tree grew in the upper world. Its roots reached down into the lower world where the swimming animals lived.

The upper world was a peaceful place until the sky chief's young wife became ill. The medicine man prayed and brought her potions to drink that should have cured her, but nothing helped.

One night, the wife dreamed that the great tree had been uprooted. When the trunk of the tree was resting on its side and the roots and branches stretched across the sky, she became well again.

Dreams were important. They foretold the future. If the chief's wife had dreamed that she would be cured if the tree were uprooted, then it must be done.

The sky people loved their tree, but they loved the chief's wife even more. They knew they had to listen to the stories from the dream world. The chief and his mightiest warriors uprooted the giant tree. An enormous hole was left in the upper world where the roots had grown. The chief carried his wife outdoors and placed her next to the hole.

Myths & Legends • EMC 759

The chief's wife heard the animals splashing in the water in the lower world. She leaned over the hole and peered into the darkness below her. She saw shadowy figures and wanted to see them more clearly. She leaned over the hole a little more and slipped into the darkness. She tumbled downward, on and on, through the black mist. The Sky Woman called to her people. They tried to reach her, but she had fallen too far.

The water animals heard Sky Woman's cries and sent two swans to catch her. The swans flew up to Sky Woman and set her on their backs. Gently they floated down to the water. All the animals came to admire the beautiful woman from the upper world.

"What shall we do with her?" asked the loon. "The swans can't carry her on their backs forever. They must look for food and care for their young. She can't live in the water as we do. She doesn't have webbed feet. It's too far to fly to the sky world to take her home."

A great turtle swam up to the swans. "I will care for Sky Woman," he said. "Set her on my back."

"That is well enough for now," said the beaver, "but she needs a bigger place to live. She needs dirt so she can plant and harvest her food. Her home must be larger than a turtle's back."

"There is only one place where we can find dirt. There is land under the water, but it's so far down that no one has ever been there," said the goose.

"Well, then," the muskrat said, "it's time someone made the trip. Who will go first?"

"I'm on my way!" said the beaver. He dove below the surface. The animals watched for his return, but he didn't come back.

"I'll go see what happened," said the otter. "Beaver can't stay under the water this long. While I'm there, I'll find dirt for Sky Woman." The otter dove into the water. The animals waited. She didn't return.

"It was my idea," said the muskrat. "I must see what has happened to my friends. I'll dive all the way to the bottom and find the dirt for Sky Woman before I return." Down he went.

After the muskrat left, the beaver came to the surface. "I dove as far as I could, but I couldn't hold my breath long enough to reach the bottom. I had to come back without the dirt."

Next came the otter. She was almost dead. "I dove until the pain was so great I had to come back. No one can dive far enough to reach the dirt."

The animals waited and circled the water where the muskrat had gone down. They had given up hope of seeing their friend again, when his head bobbed out of the water.

"Is he alive?" asked the loon.

Muskrat was out of breath and he couldn't answer. He opened his paw. Inside was a ball of dirt. The loon took the dirt and gave it to Sky Woman. She spread a bit of dirt around the edge of the turtle's shell. The turtle's shell grew bigger. Sky Woman spread more dirt on the shell until it grew into a great island.

Sky Woman felt well again. She built a lodge on the island and lived there happily with the animals.

Not too long after that, the sun, moon, and stars were created, bringing light to the lower world. Sky Woman never found a way to return to her home in the sky, but she was content with the island she had created.

       Myths & Legends • EMC 759

Name _____

Questions about
The Sky Woman

1. How was the world divided in the beginning?

_____

_____

2. Why did the sky people uproot the tree?

_____

_____

3. Who was the hero of this story? Give examples from the story that support your opinion.

_____

_____

_____

_____

4. Does this myth have a happy ending? Tell why you think as you do.

_____

_____

_____

_____

Name _____

The Sky Woman
Vocabulary

A. Write each word below on the line in front of its definition.

separated   potions   foretold   content   veil

webbed   harvest   peered   uprooted   loon

1. _____ liquid medicines

2. _____ a diving bird

3. _____ predicted

4. _____ divided

5. _____ a piece of net or fabric that conceals or protects

6. _____ satisfied

7. _____ to pick

8. _____ with skin filling the spaces between the toes

9. _____ looked searchingly

10. _____ pulled out of the ground

B. Use words from the list above to complete these sentences.

1. She must plant and _____ her food.

2. The two worlds were _____ by a _____ of darkness.

3. The Onondaga people believed that dreams _____ the future.

4. Swans have _____ feet.

Name _____

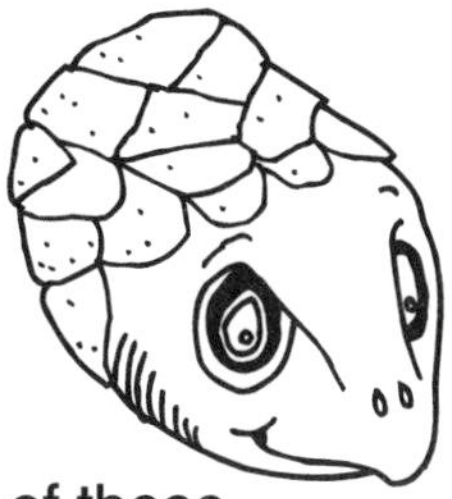

The Sky Woman
Recalling Details

Many animals helped Sky Woman in this myth. Give specific examples of how each of these animals helped.

1. **the swans:** _____

_____

2. **the turtle:** _____

_____

3. **the muskrat:** _____

_____

● ● ● Fantasy ● ● ●

Myths often involve fantasy. Give two examples of fantastic happenings in *The Sky Woman*.

_____

_____

_____

_____

_____

_____

_____

Name _____

The Sky Woman
Setting

Describe in words the world as it is presented in this myth. Then draw a picture that shows all you know about the place where the myth takes place.

_____

_____

_____

_____

_____

Answer Key

Page 7

1. Arachne could weave beautiful pictures.
2. Answers may vary. One possible answer: Arachne told the nymph that no one, goddess or mortal, could compare her work to Arachne's work.
3. Minerva was the patron of weaving.
4. Minerva wanted to teach Arachne a lesson.
5. While both tapestries were beautiful, in Minerva's tapestry the sea, the earth, and the gods seemed alive.
6. Minerva threw the shuttle at Arachne's head. Arachne shrunk into a spiderlike creature, and Minerva told her that she would have to spin webbing the rest of her life.
7. After the contest, Arachne had four long, thin legs on each side of her small round body. She spun webs in dark corners and scurried to hide.

Page 8

Arachne—talented, boastful, proud, self-centered, confident, indignant

Minerva—talented, forgiving, respectful, proud, confident, indignant

Paragraphs will vary, but should point out that while both characters were talented, proud, and confident, Arachne demonstrated disrespect and was self-centered. Pushed to her limits of tolerance, Minerva hoped to teach the boastful weaver respect and gratitude.

Page 9

A. 3
   1
   4
   2
B. 1. delicate tapestry
   2. vengeful
   3. shriveled
   4. transformed
   5. portrayed

Page 10

Sentences will vary. Possible answers:
1. After the budget cuts, the art teacher's job was hanging by a thread.
2. Tommy was flying high when he looked at the A + on his paper.
3. Jose's friendship with Ahmed was building a bridge between their two families.

Page 13

1. Echo loved to gossip, so she was never silent.
2. Juno became angry with Echo and took away her voice.
3. Narcissus loved himself.
4. Narcissus forgot to eat or drink. He became ill and died.
5. This myth is a tragedy. Both the main characters die in the sad ending.

Page 14

Definitions will vary.
1. *Echo* means "repetition of a sound caused by the reflection of sound waves."
2. *Narcissism* means "loving or worshipping oneself."

   7
   10
   9
   6
   8
   3
   5
   1
   2
   4

Page 15

1. **Positive or Neutral Connotation**—fragrance, dream, noteworthy, famous, petite, proud, generous, lovely
   Negative Connotation—soiled, nightmare, odor, ugly, filthy, greedy, slanderous, opinionated, conceited, puny
2. **Synonyms**: nightmare and dream, fragrance and odor, soiled and filthy, petite and puny, noteworthy and famous
3. **Antonyms**: generous and greedy, lovely and ugly

Page 16

Stories will vary.

Page 20

1. Jason had returned to reclaim the throne.
2. King Pelias wanted Jason to prove his bravery. He sent him to demand the return of the Golden Fleece from the King of Colchis.
3. King Pelias hoped that Jason would fail so that he himself could remain as king.

4. Jason freed Phineus from the Harpies, navigated the crashing islands, hitched fire-breathing bulls to the plow, defeated the soldiers that sprang from the dragon's teeth, and took the fleece away from a sleeping dragon.
5. crashing islands—dove fire-breathing bulls—oil fierce dragon—sleeping potion warriors in the field—magic charm

Page 21

Jason was honest. He told King Pelias why he was in his kingdom and never deceived the people he encountered on his quest.

King Pelias was dishonest. He didn't want to turn his kingdom over to Jason, so he tried to destroy him by sending him on an impossible quest.

Phineus was honest. He was so thankful to Jason for saving him from the Harpies that he warned him about the crashing islands.

King of Colchis was dishonest. He didn't intend to give Jason the Golden Fleece even if Jason was able to complete the tasks given to him.

Medea was dishonest. She tricked King Pelias's daughters into killing their father.

Page 22

1. sandals
2. King Pelias
3. King Pelias, Jason
4. ship, *Argo*
5. Phineus, Harpies
6. crashing islands
7. harness fire-breathing bulls, plant a field with dragon's teeth
8. Jason, magic charm, special oil
9. Golden Fleece
10. his crown OR his kingdom
11. killed their father
12. went up in flames
13. killed Jason
14. constellation

Page 23

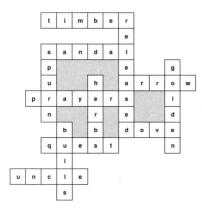

Page 27

1. Summaries will vary, but should include the following main ideas:
   Orpheus, a talented musician, fell in love with Eurydice.
   On their wedding day, Eurydice was bitten by a poisonous snake and died.
   Orpheus traveled to the Land of the Dead to beg Hades for Eurydice's return.
   When Orpheus played his music for Hades and Persephone, they agreed to release Eurydice on the condition that Orpheus not look back at her as she followed him from the Kingdom of the Dead.
   Orpheus did look back. Eurydice was returned to the Land of the Dead.
   Orpheus grieved for Eurydice.
   The nymphs grew so tired of his sad songs that they killed him.
   Orpheus and Eurydice were reunited in the Land of the Dead.
2. Orpheus charmed Hades with his songs.
3. Answers may vary. Orpheus was curious about how Eurydice had changed after her stay in the Land of the Dead. Orpheus was so close to the sunlight that he turned to make sure that Eurydice was following him.
4. Answers may vary. Some students will believe that the story was sad since both Orpheus and Eurydice were killed. Others will believe that the story ended happily because the two lovers were finally reunited.

Page 28

1. Descriptions will vary.
   Orpheus was a talented musician who demonstrated devotion to his true love. He was willing to sacrifice all to rescue her from the Land of the Dead, but wasn't able to complete the rescue because he looked back. Recognizing his own failure, he grieved for his lost love.
2. Definitions and sentences will vary.
   Persistent means "to continue with resolve." Orpheus was persistent. He insisted that Zeus let him go to the Land of the Dead to find Eurydice.

   Devoted means "showing loyalty." Orpheus was devoted. He grieved for Eurydice from morning to night.

   Unfeeling means "lacking sympathy." Orpheus was not unfeeling. His songs brought happiness to many in the Land of the Dead.
3. Responses will vary.

Page 29

1. **Happy Words**—enchanted, serenaded, lulled, charmed, peace, happiness, sunlight
   Sad Words—cried, mourned, lamented, sorrow, foolishness
2. charmed
3. lamented

Page 30

1. fair
2. Mark
3. release
4. fair
5. mark
6. release

4
2
3
5
1

Page 34

1. Pandora was almost perfect because the gods had given her many gifts.
2. Jupiter cautioned Pandora never to open the chest and to keep it locked forever.
3. When many of her visitors asked about the chest and urged her to open it, Pandora became curious.

4. Epimetheus advised Pandora to forget the chest and take a walk in the woods.
5. When Pandora opened the chest, every kind of evil flew out.
6. Hope also flew out of the chest.
7. Answers will vary, but should refer to the inclusion of Hope in the chest.

Page 35

1. Jupiter told Pandora never to open the chest.
2. Jupiter's warning let the reader know that something terrible might be in the chest and that Pandora would probably want to see what it was.

1. A "Pandora's box" is an unknown that is best left unexplored.
2. Answers will vary. A deserted mine shaft might be considered a "Pandora's box." An old family argument might be a "Pandora's box."

Page 36

A. 1. The insects represent unhappiness like sorrow, pain, evil, greed, envy, and despair.
2. Hope is being compared to a butterfly.
B. Comparisons and sentences will vary.

Page 40

1. Venus was jealous of Psyche's beauty. Venus became angry with Psyche and ordered her son to give Psyche a potion so that she would fall in love with a monster.
2. Cupid thought that Psyche was beautiful. He fell in love with Psyche when one of his arrows accidentally pierced his foot.
3. Psyche's parents were told that Psyche would become the bride of a monster.
4. Psyche's husband was kind. They laughed and sang together and he told her stories about the gods. But Psyche never saw her husband. He left each morning and returned each evening when it was dark.
5. Cupid thought that Psyche was trying to hurt him with the knife.
6. Psyche asked Venus for forgiveness. She completed impossible tasks that Venus

assigned to her. Finally, she searched for Cupid and begged him to forgive her.

Page 41

Psyche was climbing a high hill.
Venus put a slippery rock in her path.
Psyche fell and tumbled down the slope.
Cupid called to the wind to save Psyche.
The wind caught Psyche and laid her gently on a flowering meadow.
When Psyche awoke, she saw a palace.
At night Psyche heard another voice.
Psyche married the mysterious visitor.
Psyche betrayed her husband by looking at his face.

Page 42

A. 1. generous
   2. mortal
   3. sorrow
   4. haste
   5. insistence
   6. oracle
   7. quiver
   8. potion
B. 1. sorrow
   2. generous
   3. haste, quiver
   4. insistence

Page 46

1. Perseus vowed to kill the monster Medusa to repay Polydectes for his care.
2. Minerva gave him a shield, a sword, and a bag. Mercury gave Perseus winged shoes.
3. Medusa, Atlas, a sea monster, Phineus
4–6. Answers will vary, but should be reasonably justified.

Page 47

Definitions will vary.
1. jabbed — stuck into
2. summoned — asked to come
3. reflected — showed an image of
4. embraced — hugged
5. avoided — stayed away from
6. bragged — boasted
7. vowed — promised
8. lunged — moved forward suddenly

Page 48

A. 1. noun
   2. verb
   3. noun

4. verb
5. verb
6. noun
7. verb
8. noun
B. Sentences will vary. Some examples:
   1. The students must do their <u>work</u>. (noun)
      The farmer will <u>work</u> hard. (verb)
   2. The <u>drop</u> of rain fell on the blossom. (noun)
      I'm afraid he will <u>drop</u> the glass. (verb)
   3. Mrs. Brickley gave me a <u>look</u> that meant "Be quiet." (noun)
      I will <u>look</u> for the lost kitten. (verb)

Page 49

Character traits and sentences will vary.
Medusa—beautiful, boastful, dangerous, deadly
Atlas—strong, huge, conscientious
Sea Serpent—cruel, scaly, fire-breathing, scary
Perseus—brave, grateful, kind, skilled fighter

Page 53

1. changes in growing things caused by the seasons
2. Pluto planned to kidnap Proserpina and take her to his kingdom.
3. The ground dried up and all the plants turned brown.
4. Proserpina had drunk the juice from pomegranate seeds while she was in the World of the Dead.
5. Answers will vary. Although Pluto is the King of the Underworld and kidnaps Proserpina, he demonstrates kindness toward her and accepts Jupiter's compromise, so students can make a case for both evil and good.
6. Answers will vary.

Page 54

A. 1. precious
   2. cavern
   3. dreary
   4. pomegranate
   5. chasm
   6. tend
   7. offerings
   8. grieves
   9. frantically
   10. chariot
B. 1. miserable, precious, dreary, cavern

2. chariot, chasm
3. tend, grieves

Page 55

Answers will vary. Some examples:
Blessings—new growth, blooming flowers, leaves on the trees, green grass, etc.
Forgetfulness—bare trees; dry, brown grass; barren hills

Page 56

Writing will vary.

Page 60

1. King Minos captured the dreaded Minotaur. He demanded hostages from Athens to feed the Minotaur.
2. The Minotaur was a monster with a human body and the head of a bull. It had a huge appetite and loved to eat people.
3. Theseus believed that if he killed the Minotaur, then no more Athenians would have to be sacrificed.
4. Ariadne gave Theseus a magic ball of string so he could escape from the labyrinth.
5. Daedalus warned Icarus not to fly too close to the sun because the sun's rays would melt the wax that held the wings together.
6. Answers will vary. You could use Super Glue™ instead of wax.

Page 61

A. 2
   1
   4
   6
   7
   3
   8
   9
   5
B–D. Sentences will vary.

Page 62

1. Daedalus and a mother bird
2. Writing will vary.

1. the wind
2. a magic ball of string

Page 63

Opinions will vary. Student responses should be considered correct if they are logically supported with examples from the myth.

Page 64

Page 70
1. Thor and Skrymir are the two main characters.
2. Skrymir described the hammer blows as acorns and leaves falling on his head.
3. Thialfi said that he was the fastest runner in Midgard. Loki said that he could eat more than any giant. Thor said that he could drink more than anyone.
4. Skrymir disguised himself and acted as the travelers' guide.
   He only pretended to sleep.
   He took the travelers' food. When the travelers arrived in the giant's city, Skrymir set up impossible tasks. Thialfi raced against Thought. Loki tried to eat faster than Fire. Thor tried to drink the sea dry and wrestled Old Age.
5. Skrymir and his city disappeared.

Page 71
A. 1. survived
   2. appeared
   3. stumbled
   4. humiliated
   5. floored
   6. defeated
   7. failed
   8. hobbled
   9. disappeared
   10. challenged
B. Sentences will vary.

Page 72
Old Age becomes an old woman. Old age is inevitable. It happens to everyone regardless of their strength or their size. So no one defeats old age.

Thought becomes a swift runner. A man's thinking can move faster than his feet. So thinking wins the race against running.
Fire becomes a hungry giant. Fire can consume wood, bones, and meat. So in an eating contest with fire, even a hungry man loses.

Page 73
1. The travelers had to run to keep up with Skrymir.
2. The gates touched the clouds.
3. Thor's hammer blows made deep valleys in the earth.

1. Answers will vary. Skrymir seems to be insulting Thor.
2. Answers will vary. Skrymir recognizes Thor's strength when he rolls away from each of the hammer blows. At the end of the story, he admits that the hammer blows would have killed him.

Page 77
1. Answers will vary. Some students may see Loki as a friend because he gave Mjollnir to Thor and negotiated with the giants. Others may not consider Loki a friend because he turned himself into a hawk and flew away, leaving Thor to fight the giants alone.
2. Loki gave him the hammer.
3. The giants could not win battles against Thor as long as he had Mjollnir.
4. Loki had Thor disguise himself as Freyja and agree to marry Thrym in exchange for the hammer.
5. Thrym thought his bride wore large boots and had a giant appetite and red eyes.

Page 78
A. 1. ransom
   2. tresses
   3. pleaded
   4. reluctantly
   5. mischievous
   6. bargain
   7. in favor of
   8. forged
   9. practical
   10. culprit
B. 1. practical
   2. tresses
   3. ransom
   4. bargain
   5. reluctantly
   6. forged

Page 79
6
1
8
7
2
3
4
9
10
5

Opinions about the most significant event of the story should be well supported.

Page 80
Definitions and sentences will vary.

replace = to place again
Please replace the books after you have finished reading.

return = to come again
I will return after I have finished my work.

reread = to read again
I can't wait to reread the ending of the story.

refund = to pay again (back)
The store will refund the full amount if you take the shirt back.

unconscious = not conscious
The boy was unconscious after the accident.

unaware = not aware
The driver was unaware of the accident up ahead.

uncertain = not certain
The outcome of the vote was uncertain.

unbroken = not broken
The cookies arrived unbroken.

Page 84
1. Balder was afraid that he would die soon.
2. Odin visited a soul that could foresee the future. The soul said that nothing could be done to change the future. Frigg traveled throughout the nine worlds and made everything promise to protect Balder.

3. Hoder killed Balder. The gods blamed Loki because Hoder was blind and Loki handed Hoder the pointed mistletoe stick and showed Hoder how to aim it.
4. If every creature wept for Balder, Hel would release Balder from Niflheim.
5. Loki disguised himself as a giantess and refused to cry. Then he hid from the gods by changing shape whenever the gods were near.

Page 85
A. 1. Hel
2. Hoder
3. Odin
4. Loki
5. Balder
6. Ragnarok
B. Classifications may vary. They should be considered correct if they are logically explained.

Hel	good	Hel agreed to release Balder if everything in all nine worlds wept for him.
Balder	good	Balder was the kindest and the most beloved Norse god.
Frigg	good	Frigg tried to protect her son from harm.
Loki	bad	Loki caused Balder's death and almost caused the agreement with Hel to fail.
Odin	good	Odin rode to Niflheim to get advice for Balder.

Page 86
A. 6
2
8
1
4
3
5
7
9

B. Students may choose different story events. They might, for example, choose:
Odin rides to Niflheim to visit a soul who could foretell the future. The event comes between event number 1 and event number 2.

Page 87
A. 8
1
2
7
10
5
4
6
9
3
B. 1. assured
2. pierced
3. envied
4. prophecy
C. Sentences will vary.

Page 92
1. Opinions will vary, but should be justified. For example: I believe that Gilgamesh and Enkidu were friends because Gilgamesh grieved for Enkidu when he was killed. OR Gilgamesh and Enkidu were not friends because Enkidu was not honest with Gilgamesh. Enkidu didn't let Gilgamesh know how strong he was.
2. Gilgamesh was a great warrior and a great builder. He wanted to accomplish great things. He was strong and handsome. Gilgamesh had little empathy for those around him. He overworked his people. He was self-centered and often took on more than he could do by himself.
3. Enkidu insulted Ishtar and the other gods and goddesses. He helped Gilgamesh kill the Bull of Heaven.
4. He became ill and died. Students' opinions on whether the punishment was justified may vary. One example might be: Enkidu was only trying to protect his friend from an unjust attack. He was only guilty of losing his temper, so I think the punishment was unjust.
5. He wanted to do great deeds so that people would remember him after his death.

Page 93
1. f
b
d
a
e
c
2. Before he met Enkidu, Gilgamesh was driven to build new projects. He always won every battle.
3. After he met Enkidu, Gilgamesh had someone his equal to battle. The king's adventures with Enkidu kept him busy so that he didn't start so many projects. He followed the traditions of his people so that Enkidu could understand them.
4. Sentences will vary. One example might be: Meeting Enkidu calmed Gilgamesh and provided an outlet for his energy and drive.

Page 94
A. 6
1
5
4
3
7
2
10
8
11
9
12
B. 1. gazelle
2. stacked
3. overworked
4. adventures

Page 95
Writing will vary.

Page 99
1. The sun traveled so fast across the sky that the people didn't have time to finish their work.
2. Hina-of-the-Fire said that the sun travels fast because he always had. She said that he wouldn't change—that he would do only what pleased him.
3. Maui's grandmother thought he could change the sun because he could change the sky.
4. He caught the sun in a strong net.
5. The sun agreed to go slowly for one-half of the year.
6. The myth explains why summer has longer days.

Page 100
1. a. The sun moved so fast, he didn't answer the people's prayers.
   b. The sun let off a fiery glow and hurried on his way without answering.
   c. The sun scorched Maui and tried to burn everything around him.
2. The sun talked.
   The sun agreed to the bargain.

Page 101
Definitions may vary. Some examples:
1. You have behaved badly.
   behaved badly means "misbehaved"
2. Maui's mother, Hina-of-the-Fire, complained because the days were too short.
   complained means "protested"
3. As each ray climbed out of the sea, it was entangled.
   entangled means "tangled up or trapped"
4. She sets out an offering of fruit for him each morning.
   sets out means "puts out"
5. To show her how clever he was, Maui drew a rainbow across the sky.
   clever means "skilled"
6. They were always hungry and ill-tempered.
   ill-tempered means "out of sorts"

Page 102
Circled words should include negotiator, thoughtful, contemplative, willing to ask for advice, popular, polite, determined.

Paragraphs will vary, but should include justification.

Page 105
1. The two brothers couldn't agree on anything.
2. Mawu told her two sons that she would not take either side and that the two would have to learn to get along.
3. Sagbata's exit did not help the brothers get along. Sogbo withheld rain from the Earth because his brother was there.
4. It is important to learn to get along with the people around you. Removing yourself from a situation doesn't always solve the problem.
5. Opinions will vary. One example might be:

I think that Mawu was right in the way she dealt with her sons because solving the problem for her sons would not help them learn how to solve their problems.

Page 106
Definitions and examples may vary.
Revenge means "a punishment inflicted because of something that has happened before."
Sogbo withheld the rain from the Earth as revenge because Sagbata had taken all of the treasures.

Reconciliation means "getting back together and restoring friendship."
Sagbata offered to share leadership of the Earth with Sogbo in the hope of reconciliation.

Student examples of revenge and reconciliation in their experience will vary.

Page 107
A. de—do the opposite of
mis—badly or wrongly
un—not
re—back or again
B. Sentences, synonyms, and antonyms will vary.
1. The climber will descend using the rope.
   climb down—climb up
2. It was her misfortune to have lost her purse.
   bad luck—good luck
3. It is always unwise to walk alone after dark.
   foolish—smart
4. I will return the library book tomorrow.
   take back—check out

Page 108
Creative descriptions will vary.

Page 112
1. The sun children had the bodies of birds. They perched in the branches of a giant mulberry tree until it was their turn to drive the chariot that moved across the sky each day.
2. The sun children became bored with their daily routine. They all jumped into the chariot at one time. Their combined heat was too hot for the Earth.

3. The people told him that there would be nothing left for him to rule if he did not act quickly.
4. Being without any sunlight is worse than having too much sunlight.

Page 113
Descriptions and opinions will vary. The description of the mother might include characteristics such as caring, organized, ineffective, a pushover.

The description of the father might include characteristics such as out of touch, formal, a figurehead.

Page 114
A. elephant—plod, trumpet, splash
lion—roar, stalk, hunt
antelope—leap, flee, graze
monkey—tease, swing, scramble, hang
B. Writing will vary.

Page 115
Sentences will vary. Some examples:
1. The hunter carried his arrows in a quiver. (noun)
   My knees began to quiver as I waited for the announcement. (verb)
2. The fire crackled in the dark night. (noun)
   The boss will fire him for insubordination. (verb)
3. We need to have a talk about that problem. (noun)
   Who will talk to the ball team? (verb)
4. His aim is very good. (noun)
   Aim the arrow at the bull's-eye. (verb)
5. I raised my hand to answer. (noun)
   I will hand in my paper tomorrow. (verb)

Page 119
1. In the beginning the universe was a great void. There were no birds, fish, crabs, trees, rocks, holes, canyons, straw, or reeds. There was no noise. The lifeless sea floated through space.
2. The Creator hoped that the new creature would sing his praises.
3. a. The mud creatures were too soft.
      They were destroyed.
   b. The wood creatures were unfeeling and not very smart.

Most of the wood people were destroyed by the other creatures in the world. The few remaining were changed into monkeys.

c. The corn people were too perfect. They saw and knew everything. The Creator fogged their eyes so they saw less and didn't know everything.

Page 120
8
1
7
2
6
5
10
4
9
3

Page 121
1. **Mud People**—dissolved in water, too soft, first people created, made noise but couldn't think
   Wood People—unfeeling, expressions never changed, their words had no meaning, turned into monkeys
   Corn People—strong and healthy, too perfect, ancestors of human race
2. Descriptions will vary, but should include the characteristics listed in the columns.

Page 122
A. 1. collapsed
   2. grateful
   3. ancestors
   4. lifeless
   5. void
   6. expression
   7. perfect
   8. incense
B. 1. ancestors
   2. expression
   3. void
   4. collapsed
   5. grateful

Page 126
1. Sedna wanted a husband who was rich, handsome, and very generous.
2. The seabird changed into a man and promised her a warm house and lots of food.
3. Sedna's father visited her the summer after she left with her new husband. When Sedna begged him to rescue her, he killed the seabird and paddled out to sea with Sedna in his kayak. The other birds created a stormy sea and threatened the pair. Sedna's father threw her overboard in the icy waters and would not let her return to the kayak until the seabirds had flown away. When the birds had returned to their island, Sedna's father pulled her back into his kayak.
4. Sometimes sea animals are plentiful and sometimes they are scarce. The story of *Sedna, Goddess of the Sea* explains this phenomenon.

Page 127
A. **Sedna** (circled)—hard to please, fingerless, beautiful, considers self better than others, easily convinced
   seabird (underlined)—artist of disguise, deceitful, jealous
   Sedna's father (boxed)—careful, wise, skeptical
B. Descriptions will vary.

Page 128
A. 2
   4
   1
   8
   6
   5
   3
   7
B. Sentences will vary. Some examples:
   1. The groom waited at the front of the church for the bride.
      The stable boy will groom the horses in the evening.
   2. I broke a bone in my arm skiing.
      The well is bone dry.
      Help me bone the fish before I eat it.

Page 129
Promise 1—Come with me to a warmer land where you will not have to work.
The winds blew as fiercely as they had around Sedna's old home. Sedna's bird husband wanted her to groom his feathers.

Promise 2—You'll sleep in a warm bearskin bed in my fur tent.
The fur tent was a smelly house made of fish skins. The bed was a hard mat covered with damp feathers.

Promise 3—You'll never be hungry again.
The birds fought over each scrap of raw fish. They pecked at Sedna when she took a piece for herself.

Promise 4—The birds will see you have everything you need.
Sedna is told to be content. The birds steal most of her clothes.

Page 133
1. The two worlds were separated by a veil of darkness.
2. The chief's wife had dreamed that she would be cured if the great tree was uprooted.
3. Answers will vary. Some examples: The beaver can be considered a hero because it thinks of a plan to save Sky Woman. The muskrat can be considered a hero because it is able to bring the ball of dirt to the surface. The turtle can be considered a hero because it provides the surface for Sky Woman's island.
4. Opinions may differ. The myth has a happy ending because the animals of the water world make a safe home for Sky Woman. She gets well and lives happily with the animals. Some students may think that the myth has an unhappy ending because Sky Woman never finds a way to return to her home in the sky.

Page 134
A. 1. potions
   2. loon
   3. foretold
   4. separated
   5. veil
   6. content
   7. harvest
   8. webbed
   9. peered
   10. uprooted
B. 1. harvest
   2. separated, veil
   3. foretold
   4. webbed

Page 135

1. The swans caught Sky Woman when she fell from the upper world. They carried her on their backs.
2. The turtle cared for Sky Woman. He carried her on his back. When the soil was placed around the edge of his shell, his shell grew into an island.
3. The muskrat dove to the bottom of the water and brought a ball of dirt to the surface for Sky Woman.

Two possible examples of fantasy are:
The animals talked.
The turtle's shell grew into an island.

Page 136

Descriptions and drawings will vary.